Teach with Confidence

Five Domains for Managing Life in Classrooms

Alexandra Miletta

ROWMAN & LITTLEFIELD
Lanham • Boulder • New York • London

Published by Rowman & Littlefield
An imprint of The Rowman & Littlefield Publishing Group, Inc.
4501 Forbes Boulevard, Suite 200, Lanham, Maryland 20706
www.rowman.com

86-90 Paul Street, London EC2A 4NE

British Library Cataloguing in Publication Information available

Library of Congress Cataloging-in-Publication Data
Names: Miletta, Alexandra, author.
Title: Teach with confidence : five domains for managing life in classrooms / Alexandra Miletta.
Description: Lanham, Maryland : Rowman & Littlefield, 2024. | Includes bibliographical references and index.
Identifiers: LCCN 2024016836 (print) | LCCN 2024016837 (ebook) | ISBN 9781538194973 (hardcover) | ISBN 9781538194980 (paperback) | ISBN 9781538194997 (epub)
Subjects: LCSH: Classroom management. | Teacher-student relationships. | Confidence.
Classification: LCC LB3013 .M53 2024(print) | LCC LB3013(ebook) | DDC 371.102/3—dc23/eng/20240531
LC record available at https://lccn.loc.gov/2024016836
LC ebook record available at https://lccn.loc.gov/2024016837

™ The paper used in this publication meets the minimum requirements of American National Standard for Information Sciences—Permanence of Paper for Printed Library Materials, ANSI/NISO Z39.48-1992.

Contents

Acknowledgments

I WISH TO THANK MANY PEOPLE WHO HAVE ASSISTED ME IN bringing this work to completion. My editor, Nathan Davidson, for his assistance and encouragement, was all one could hope for in an editorial professional. My good friend and dissertation partner, Kathy Morris, provided early support and her home when I needed a retreat, and has been steadfast in her ability to listen to my ideas, my complaints, my fears and get me through it all. My former student Angelica Kennedy provided excellent feedback on an early draft. My colleagues and friends Cindy Ballenger and Dirck Roosevelt have mentored me, collaborated with me, and believed in me. I aspire to their level of intellectual rigor and compassion. My talented artist friend in Rome, Chiara Pasqualotto, made the beautiful drawing on the cover and also illustrates children's picture books. The many former students who allowed me to use their writing and their stories, and parents who gave permission to use photographs of their children, have my deepest gratitude. Finally, I am grateful to my sister Jennifer, her husband David, and their children Felix and Annabelle, for being my family and providing their expertise when needed. I dedicate this book to my mother, Maureen, an advocate for uncertainty.

Introduction

Entering the Maze

Browsing through my mother's books one summer shortly after I started teaching, I found Caroline Pratt's *I Learn From Children* (1948). In her foreword she wrote:

> *What I know of children I have learned from them. There have been moments when I have felt like Columbus discovering a new continent, and, conversely, many times when the uncharted world of childhood has presented no clear path by which a mere adult could find her way in it. (p. 9)*

Be thinking about what you know about children from experiences you have had. It seems to me a perfect way for us to begin.

"Classroom management" is a ubiquitous term in education. It can mean many things and is used in multiple contexts. Sometimes it seems to refer to something a teacher possesses, as in "she has good classroom management" or, more broadly, "first year teachers need to work on their classroom management." In print it often refers to techniques, methods, and systems. A search on the internet will turn up more than a million hits and endless sponsored links promising ways to control the toughest students with research-proven and easy-to-adopt strategies. At times, classroom management seems to refer to something quite tangible, such as an attendance procedure or directions given to students to transition from one thing to the next. Other times, it is more ephemeral and all-encompassing, referring to student motivation, classroom climate, pacing of lessons, and the extent to which students are engaged in a task. Teacher folklore warns not to smile until December, because teachers are often judged by their sternness and how well they can control misbehavior, both commonly equated with classroom management.

So, if classroom management is seemingly everywhere, why does it continue to be such an elusive thing to understand and acquire, especially for beginning teachers? Why do so many graduates of teacher education programs complain that they learned nothing about classroom management in their courses? Moreover, why does classroom management seem to be a cause of the despair and malaise suffered by so many hardworking new teachers? Perhaps some of these conceptions of classroom management and how to improve one's classroom management skills are misguided. I believe it is misleading to tell beginning teachers that it is possible to adopt a universal approach to classroom management that will work in any classroom context. Perhaps behind the seemingly good intentions of those promising solutions to classroom management problems lies a desire to profit from the market's demand.

Classroom management has become a growth industry over the past two decades. Teachers and administrators are bombarded with advice, programs, videos, discipline strategies, and research findings. Districts are urged to spend money on the latest gadgets, clickers, point systems, smart board and computer programs, and professional development guaranteed to improve that ever-elusive goal of "time on task." Yet teachers routinely report that persistent problems with classroom management and discipline are key reasons why they leave the profession. Whatever they have tried simply isn't working.

This book is written to guide teachers* through the classroom management maze, to provide insights into the work of managing life in classrooms through the domains of planning, reflecting, knowing students, collaborating, and theorizing in this uniquely challenging time for educators. Unlike books with the latest tips and strategies, readers will find here ways to pay attention to their own contexts, maintaining complexity and nuance rather than reducing or ignoring it, and to understand the classroom climate and culture that is being constructed by its members. The goal is to help new teachers understand the value of five key actions teachers can work on that, in my experience at least, are critical domains of good and successful work in teaching:

---

*I use this word to be inclusive of all educators, but my primary audience is intended to be those who are preservice teachers through their first two years of teaching. Student teachers are those who are working with a mentor teacher and are finishing their teacher preparation coursework.

1. Plan and be prepared.
2. Reflect, evaluate, learn.
3. Know students and their families.
4. Collaborate with and trust colleagues.
5. Be cognizant of the theories, research, and ideas that inform their practice.

Approaches to classroom management that fail to take contexts into account offer advice that may or may not succeed in achieving desired goals. This book takes a culturally responsive approach premised on the belief that teachers can be more successful when they truly know and understand their students and their needs. I use the concept of classroom management broadly, to encompass beliefs, knowledge, and skill in building relationships. I believe a teacher needs a full repertoire of strategies for managing the diversity found in all classrooms. While that often comes with experience gained from making mistakes and an ongoing assessment of what works, what doesn't, and why, there are also ways to be strategic about studying students and reflecting on practice from the moment you step into a classroom that can make you a better and more effective teacher, and help you in building relationships based on mutual trust and respect.

Chapter 1 describes some of my own personal learning experiences and history, and the wise elders that inform my beliefs and philosophy of teaching and working with student teachers in classrooms. I also describe my research interests and experiences as a teacher educator that have helped shape the ideas presented and the practices I have invested in over the years. I have on-the-ground experience in urban and suburban schools, and knowledge of the research literature on supervision and teacher learning, that inform my ideas about what serves beginning teachers well and sets them on a path to success.

In this chapter I will also explain the framework that uses classroom management, defined to include the notion of managing and using dilemmas, as a lens through which one can examine five key domains of the work of teaching. In my own ethnographic research, I have explored how expert teachers managed the ongoing dilemmas of practice, at times using the tensions they experienced intentionally as opportunities to support their students' learning. In light of their academic, social, and civic goals and specific aims located within those goals, as well as knowledge of their students, they drew on previous experience to weigh the benefits and drawbacks of possible courses of action. These domains of the work of managing life in classrooms are not necessarily new. My approach and use of them in

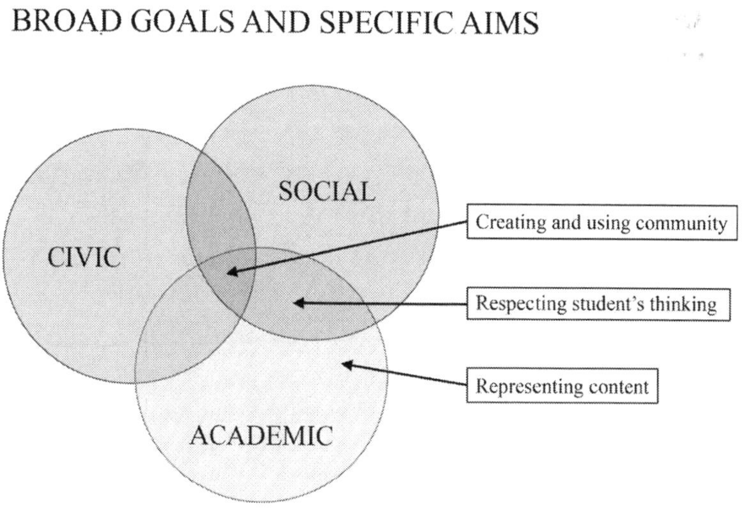

this framework for beginning teachers is quite different from extant classroom management advice, however, and I believe these five domains are key to building confidence and achieving success with students. Examples from cases across grades and contexts will set the stage for a more detailed look in the chapters that follow.

Next in chapter 2 I will outline a simplified way to think about lesson planning as a proactive approach to heading off discipline problems before they happen. A basic plan for learning has four parts:

1. Curriculum, framed as the question What do I want to teach?
2. Rationale, or Why does it matter?
3. Instruction, or How will I teach?
4. Assessment, or How will I know what students learned?

The point of this way of thinking about planning is that students need to be informed about teachers' expectations for them, and the reasons for learning the material at hand, which must also be made relevant and interesting to those particular students the teacher is charged with engaging in learning. When students understand these four features of any lesson, chances are improved for keeping everyone on track, involved and invested in the learning process and its outcomes.

Educators have always felt a tension between breadth and depth in teaching content, but recently they have less agency in managing it; too often decisions are driven by external pressures. Implementation of policies requiring greater accountability have meant that teachers, both novice and expert, were expected to follow carefully scripted curriculum aligned with detailed standards. A consequence of high-stakes testing is that subjects not tested for high-stakes purposes are losing classroom time to those that are. While learning to write and successfully execute lesson plans continues to be a focus in methods courses in most teacher preparation programs, the domain of planning has therefore become a more complex learning process for new teachers than just following a teacher guide and textbook lessons. Planning, to truly meet the needs of all learners, must entail critical examination of tensions between teaching for intellectual growth, curiosity, and understanding and teaching for the short-term goal of success on standardized tests.

Because of the unrelenting focus on narrow achievement outcomes measured by tests, which has undoubtedly had a negative effect on students' and teachers' enjoyment of school and learning in many places, teachers face additional problems related to classroom management and school climate. Important subjects such as music and physical education are being eliminated or reduced in too many schools, and homework and preparation for tests is often the focus of after-school programs, rather than extracurricular enrichment. It is therefore even more crucial for new teachers to have concrete advice about knowing students' interests and strengths in order to plan accordingly. We'll see how all of this comes together in a detailed look at the planning and teaching of one of my student teachers.

Student teachers also need to learn that reflecting on what went wrong is as important as acknowledging what went well. Chapter 3 will explore how to develop skills of reflection and evaluation. Although reflective practice has become a common term, teachers are often told to reflect in a journal without a clear sense of the value of such writing once they leave their teacher preparation programs. This book uses the strategy of focusing on a single episode of classroom life to construct a research story, sometimes called a well-remembered event (Carter, 1993). These are used to guide teachers in describing, analyzing, and interpreting brief memorable stories that are especially meaningful to them. These research stories can and should be shared with parents and colleagues as a way to break down the isolation of teaching and collaboratively work on solutions to recurring problems; reflection is a social practice. One of the central goals of my teaching is to inspire new teachers to work together to manage dissonance, trust their ability to reflect and grow, and have an improved sense of their own agency in doing what is in the best interests of the students they are charged with teaching.

How do teachers learn about their students? The Descriptive Review used by Patricia Carini at the Prospect School in Vermont (Carini & Himley, 2000) provides a valuable framework for knowing and understanding students. Chapter 4 will illustrate how teachers, together with parents and colleagues who have taught students in previous years, can begin to build rich portraits that look at the whole child and not just test scores and grades. When teachers seek to know about students' interests and ways of knowing, and observe their gestures and social interactions, they open up possibilities for conversations that are vital to developing solid relationships.

This chapter also looks at the question of values and moral considerations in teaching. So much of schooling and youth athletics is dominated by the value of competition that we tend to neglect or overlook important values for living well in a participatory democracy, such as cooperation, diversity, and caring. These are values that instill a sense of the greater good and lead to a positive climate of interdependency. Learning to handle challenging behavior issues and personal conflicts that inevitably arise in classrooms requires a commitment to nurturing and modeling these values so that students can be helped to return to a feeling of normalcy when anger and frustration get out of hand.

While there is much good work for teachers to focus on in their own classrooms, school climate plays an important role as well in the health of any school. Meier's (2002) analysis of the value of trust makes it clear that without trust there can be no meaningful collaboration and collegiality in schools. In chapter 5, ways to be proactive about seeking advice and support from others, and how to make best use of that wisdom, will be explored. Beginning teachers are sometimes assigned a mentor, but are seldom shown how to go out and build relationships with colleagues just down the hall. Every teacher can benefit from knowing there is a trusted colleague nearby. Colleagues should also be more than just people who will help out in a crisis or provide some advice on solving a troubling problem. More and more schools, both in the United States and abroad, are working on developing professional learning communities to stimulate the intellectual growth of all educators and to aid teachers in learning through sustained inquiry and collaboration.

Paradoxically, while efforts are intensifying to elevate the profession of teaching by creating more rigorous standards for entry into preparation programs and more requirements for certification, teachers are often given watered-down versions of research results, particularly when it comes to classroom management. The sixth chapter reviews a variety of written genres from textbooks to accounts of teacher researchers, and explores four metaphors for conceptions of schools that emerged from research literature: the school as a military institution; school as home; school as democratic community; and school as theater. Each is examined through detailed examples to uncover the usefulness and shortcomings of these metaphors. I argue that rather than comparing sets of alternative strategies and approaches to classroom management, beginning teachers need to explore and reflect on their own metaphorical conceptions for classroom life, making important choices and decisions about organization and personal interactions among students and teachers accordingly.

Throughout the book, my aim is to take an honest look at the realities of putting these ideas into practice by combining my research on the writing of my student teachers during their field placement experiences, and some interviews on their experiences since that time as classroom teachers. Through the voices of practitioners, my hope is to help readers see how the ideas presented in these chapters can help to sustain interest in and a commitment to a lifelong career in teaching, despite ongoing challenges and obstacles. Learning to develop habits of reflection, especially as part of a community of teachers, can provide better ways to understand the students in your care and yourself as a teacher, and to address the social inequities and problems related to poverty and racism that filter into school contexts.

Chapter 1

How I Can Help You

The first time I picked up a book by John Dewey I chose *Experience and Education* (1938), which my mother assured me was one of his most readable works. In it I found this gem, which has always stayed with me:

> *Every experience is a moving force. Its value can be judged only on the ground of what it moves toward and into. (p. 38)*

How do you afford students freedom to experience things that will educate them while also directing them to make new discoveries and connect to prior knowledge?

Every one of us spends the better part of our childhoods and adolescence in school, observing teachers and classmates in action. We participate in a variety of ways, talking and doing things together with others, and we become members of a school community. Some people hate school, some love it, and most are somewhere in between. Dan Lortie, in his famous sociological study of teaching, *Schoolteacher* (1975), coined the term "apprenticeship of teaching" and argued that these early schooling experiences are largely responsible for the beliefs held by beginning teachers as they begin their studies of education. One of the more challenging aspects of learning to reflect on your teaching is being able to identify and untangle where your beliefs about teaching and learning, and your knowledge for professional practice, come from.

Many teachers are drawn to teaching as a calling because someone in their family or circle of friends was a teacher and provided an additional window into the less visible aspects of the work than that provided by the normal interactions with teachers and students in school. In my case, both my mother and her mother were teachers, and although my grandmother died right after I was born, I grew up hearing a lot about how she taught in a one-room schoolhouse in western Ireland before moving to New York. I also attended the elementary school where my mother was a teacher and was periodically recruited to help her out in the classroom. School staff parties were often held in our house, and I grew up listening to stories about teaching and school life from my mother and her teacher friends. My mother began pursuing a doctorate in education at Teachers College in New York when I was in high school, and by the time I was a senior, she had convinced me to volunteer as a teacher in her classroom twice a week. I remember guiding a small reading group through various fairy tales and teaching another group about energy. Her classroom was exceptional in that three upper elementary grades were combined and taught by three teachers, and the curriculum was organized into multiweek modules of study, with courses picked by the students (Miletta, 1996). Teaching, it seemed at the time, came naturally to me.

Supervising Student Teachers

Fast-forward in my personal biography to when I had left classroom teaching to pursue a doctorate. I was involved in supervising student teachers who were in a full-time master's program focused on urban education, what Jean Anyon (1997) more boldly called "ghetto schooling" in her book of the same title. Pushing beyond mainstream notions of the problems in inner-city schools and failed attempts at reform, Anyon spent years researching schools in Newark, New Jersey, to describe and provide insight into the painful effects of poverty and racial isolation. She made a strong case for uncovering not only the "histories of the schools and districts, but also those of the cities in which they are embedded" (p. xv) and for enabling educational reform through "economic reprioritization, and a resuscitation of the cities themselves" (p. xvi). Let's drop in on my visit to Goodman Elementary, a Detroit public school with a poverty rate of over 60%; its population is almost entirely African American.

Students are intently working on a spelling crossword as Suzanne, my student teacher, circulates. Suzanne is white, in her forties, and has a warm, calm presence. As I walk in, several children look up and smile and wave at me as I creep in through the back of the room to the table in the far corner. Suzanne smiles as she prompts them and they enthusiastically say in unison, "Good morning, Ms. M!" I smile and say good morning back, and chat briefly with Ms. Green, Suzanne's cooperating teacher, who is African American, as I settle in and open my notebook.

I immediately notice that Suzanne has stopped to say happy birthday to Dashonda, a girl sitting nearby, and she seems to glow from the special attention as she converses with Suzanne. I tend to notice these kinds of interactions more than others because in my own research I have become interested in the moral dimensions of teaching, especially how teachers grapple with moral dilemmas, as well as in how students and their teacher come together and develop social and cultural understandings and ways of being together in the crowded space of a classroom. I realize I notice certain things at the expense of others, but all observation of teaching is an interpretive act, and we all bring our experiences and our lenses to bear on our interpretations (Erickson, 1986).

The spelling words written on the board end in the letter y and are in the plural form. When Suzanne has a moment to come over as students work independently, she gives me a copy of the crossword and I ask her about the spelling rule in this pattern; then together we remember that if there's a vowel before the y you just add s for the plural, but if there's a consonant you change it to -ies. These little micro-interactions are my teachable moments; such opportunities for side conversations are very rare. I once read, much to my dismay, about a study that employed an electronic "third ear device" so that the supervisor could speak to the student teacher *while she was teaching* (Giebelhaus, 1994). With the proliferation of portable video technology, we will likely see online, remote supervision in the near future (Rodgers, 2012). I can't imagine anything more disruptive, and I am concerned about what video surveillance means for privacy. I prefer being present in the moment, always on the alert for a chance to unobtrusively point something out as it's happening: a student helping another student who's been hurt, an insightful comment, a problem solved.

Suzanne has been in charge of teaching spelling to her third graders for months now, and for each lesson creates a crossword and extra challenges for the students. They seem to absolutely love it and easily follow the familiar routine of sharing answers and spelling the words as a whole class now that they have completed the puzzle independently. Suzanne continues to move around the spaces between tables of clustered desks, sometimes reminding certain people to stay with the class as she looks over shoulders. I overhear her say, "Patricia, I never want to hear shut up. Be quiet is fine." There are no further protests from Patricia, and the lesson moves fluidly along.

One of the ways in which I look for moral dimensions of classroom life is when the teacher conveys a virtue (Fenstermacher, 2001; Richardson & Fallona, 2001; Sockett, 1993). Virtues identified by these researchers and others include honesty, caring, and open-mindedness. In this moment, however, the student is taking on the teacher's role, for I see both Patricia reminding another student (in a not-so-nice way) not to talk during work time, and the teacher reminding Patricia to be nicer about her reminder. It's worth noting that the question of virtues, specifically *whose* virtues, is a topic of heated discussion, so I must acknowledge that depending on context, "shut up" can be used in a joking way, to mean "get out" or "no way." Perhaps because there is always a certain amount of undesirable side conversations in classrooms, some teachers are a bit extra sensitive about students' use of "shut up." I know I am especially sensitive about it, because when I was a teacher, a parent complained to my principal that I had no control over my classroom and often yelled, "Shut up!" which was completely untrue. At any rate, it was interesting to me and morally significant that Suzanne was teaching Patricia to substitute "be quiet" for "shut up," explicitly attempting to instill in her the habit of using one more than the other.

The class continues to go over answers, and Suzanne reads the clue for 3 down: the first name of a famous African American woman athlete who overcame polio to become an Olympic winner. Suddenly, almost every hand in the room is stretching up and wiggling with enthusiasm, and to reinforce the significance of the answer, Suzanne writes Wilma Rudolph on the board, and I realize that they have just read her biography as a class. I am reminded of how important it is to make the content of what is being taught relevant to the students and to their experiences and interests. Suzanne then tells the students about the spelling pattern we had discussed earlier, and praises them for the ways in which they have improved in finding such patterns. This not only assists them in looking for spelling patterns in words, but the praise has the magical effect (when the students somehow know it is sincere and heartfelt) of enhancing relationships. The other important thing about this moment is that Suzanne is giving collective praise, for sometimes publicly praising individuals, or worse, awarding points for good behavior, can backfire and create animosity and resentment.

The transition from spelling to social studies flashes by in a second, and Suzanne has written the word "library" on the board, asking students why you would use a library. Students offer various ideas: to learn things, to read books, to look up and find information. Suzanne says, "We talked about a kind of book where you'd go to find information—" her voice trailing off to prompt an answer, and she calls on a student who responds, "Nonfiction?" Suzanne acknowledges, "Well, that's a category. So is fiction." Another student suggests "reference" and Suzanne says, "That's the category I was looking for." I make a mental note to myself to discuss this exchange with her, for I notice a missed opportunity to probe the student's reasons for suggesting nonfiction, which seems like a good answer to the question about the kind of book where you'd find information. I want to caution her about having "one right answer" in your head; that can block out student answers that may be logical depending on their reasoning for giving that answer. I'd like to think most of my student teachers find this sort of feedback helpful, not harsh or judgmental, and I do my best to go over my notes diplomatically. I usually begin by asking what they think went well, because their inclination is to jump right into all the things that went wrong. Traditional approaches to the post-observation conference tend to center on discussions of strengths and weaknesses, but I try instead to co-construct the events of the lesson with the student teacher so that we can build on each other's observations and thus enrich our interpretations and analysis of the teaching and learning that took place. Suzanne and others have told me that I have an effective way of conveying a suggestion or an idea that doesn't feel like criticism, so I know it is important to keep that in mind when I want to make such a point.

Sometimes I think there is no one more vulnerable than a teacher being observed, and I always try to remember the slight tremor of nervousness in my voice and the shake in my hands when my critical principal would observe me teaching my excitable sixth graders. She had a very low tolerance for even the tiniest of disruptive behaviors, like a student tapping a pencil. One time she observed me on a very hot afternoon, and hauled a boy out to the hallway, demanding an explanation for why he hadn't been paying close enough attention. "I was hot," he tried to explain in a forthright and honest way, and she actually wrote up the whole incident, including her berating of him, in my evaluation. Looking back on it I can laugh, because his comment seems so funny in the face of her authority, but at the time I was quite indignant about her treatment of him and of me.

When Suzanne asks, "Can we find entertaining books in the library?" and a student responds, "biographies," I smile to myself. I wonder if it's because reading the biography of Wilma Rudolph was entertaining. Now she is back to nonfiction, drawing a distinction between reference books and nonfiction books and holding up a book about tornadoes as an example. "Let's listen to Patricia," she gently warns as some students are talking to each other. These four simple words convey the virtue of respecting others, enhance the relationships with Patricia by reminding students her contribution matters, and develop in students the intellectual disposition of careful and attentive listening. Patricia repeats that a nonfiction book gives you information. Suzanne adds, waving the paperback in the air, "And things that really happen—do tornadoes happen?" The students enthusiastically chorus back in unison, "Yes!" Suzanne has learned to alternate between calling on students and cueing for a choral response seamlessly, and it seems to me it has the effect of keeping everyone very involved and paying attention to what is going on. I make a written note to point that out to her. Students turn to the pages of their textbook and as Rick stumbles on a name, other students jump in to help out. Suzanne takes over the reading to keep things moving along, and at one point as she circulates, holds up a book a girl is reading as an example of a fiction book. Patricia holds hers up too, and when Suzanne notices and mentions it, Patricia grins broadly. Every little bit of attention from the teacher seems to matter so much. Later in the lesson, Patricia shares an atlas as an example of a reference book, and Suzanne praises her publicly for remembering that from another lesson. Again, Patricia is beaming. Suzanne's praise always seems sincere, perhaps because she is so good at being very specific, and sometimes this praise is woven into her speech in subtle ways. She says at one point, "Someone gave me an eloquent answer to that, do you remember?" I plan to point this out to her because she may not even be aware that she is doing it or of the positive effect it appears to have on the students.

It's time to transition to a language arts lesson in which students change rooms and are grouped by reading level. "Book bag captains, you need to move fast, we're behind schedule!" Suzanne says with a cheerful, not a stressful tone, and then she holds up a book, and smiling, says to the class, "Look what Garrett still has in his book bag—Wilma Rudolph!" Now she is directing traffic, gently guiding students to the line at the door. I listen to the four book bag captains near me negotiate their task as the two girls simultaneously offer, "I'll help you" to the boys, and they answer, "We got it." Their easy rapport and enthusiasm for the job suggests a positive classroom community where helping each other is valued and recognized. However, their negotiations have slowed them down, so Ms. Green prompts them to hurry up and just get it done. Her no-nonsense tone seems to have the effect of making them hustle over to the door with all the book bags.

This time the transition takes a little longer, and Suzanne has a small group of students gathered at her feet on the rug at the other end of the room. I try to be as unobtrusive as possible because visitors from the Success for All program Goodman Elementary has adopted this year are supposed to be auditing classrooms this morning. Success for All is, in the words of its authors, "a comprehensive school-wide reform program for elementary schools serving many children placed at risk of school failure." Since its first pilot program in a Baltimore elementary school in 1987, it has expanded rapidly and is in more than 1,000 schools in 48 states (http://www.successforall.org). All classrooms at Goodman are engaged in Success for All literacy lessons every morning from 9:30 to 11:00.

Ms. Green has suggested that Suzanne read Barbara Cohen's novel *Thank You, Jackie Robinson* (1994) with students. It's about a 10-year-old Jewish boy, Sam, who befriends an older African American man, Davy, because both love the Dodgers baseball team. When Davy suffers a heart attack and lies dying in the hospital, Jackie Robinson gives Sam an autographed baseball for Davy. In a subsequent email, Suzanne told me, "Most of us got tears in our eyes when Davy passes away." She explained to me that some of the books used in Success for All are mandatory, and other parts of the curriculum allow the teacher to choose books to be read aloud. Although teachers have this element of choice, time for different parts of the lessons in each day's curriculum is carefully prescribed and allocated.

Suzanne isn't the only one of my student teachers who often feels constrained by this. They do their best to integrate ideas from their language arts methods classes at the university, but it is a challenge, particularly for the student teachers in primary grades where Success for All is even more prescriptive. Another one of my student teachers, Sarah, told me of a miscue analysis she had done with one of the highest scoring readers in her class, where she made note of words the student either couldn't read, misread, or stumbled on while reading aloud a passage of text. "She just froze when she hit words that weren't sight words or words that could be easily sounded out," Sarah lamented. "The kids are totally unprepared to deal with passages that aren't about Deena, Fran, and Sad Sam." Sarah, like others, has been questioning the usefulness of Success for All; her assessments point out what she feels are the shortcomings of the approach.

In the upper grades, 20 minutes a day are dedicated to listening comprehension. As Suzanne reads with lively expression, the students sit closely clustered on the rug, listening intently. She pauses to explain action in the story or to elaborate on the meaning of vocabulary words. When she asks them about the word usher, one student blurts out excitedly, "We have ushers at church!" The other students agree, and a girl elaborates, "Ushers can get you into the stadium or church, and greet you." Rather than interrupting the flow of the story, these temporary pauses seem to help students make meaning and relate the story to their own experiences. Suzanne is also developing certain intellectual skills in reading, showing them how to infer the meanings of unfamiliar words, how to make a picture in their minds, to predict what might happen next. When it's time to stop, the students protest in unison, "No!"

Reluctantly, they turn to more mundane exercises, reciting words and definitions in monotones.

They move to desks, and Ms. Green takes over just as the Success for All visitor arrives with the principal. Suzanne seems relieved that she isn't the one being evaluated by the auditor and comes over to sit with me at the table. The visitor, a middle-aged white woman, stays for a few minutes, reading the bulletin boards and smiling with satisfaction as she recognizes the visible signs that the program is being followed carefully. I am disappointed with this superficial evaluation and wonder if what she is checking off on her clipboard is the evidence that this teacher is adhering to the program's script. This adds to my preconceived prejudices about the Success for All program being too prescriptive and rigid, with each teacher on the same page doing the same thing on any given day. I have tried to remain open-minded about the program, for it does have good intentions, "guided by three central themes—ensuring the success of all students at key development points, building on students' personal and cultural assets, and scaling up effective programs," and it is based on rigorous research and development programs (Slavin & Madden, 1999; Slavin and colleagues, 1996). However, a teacher's account of life in a Success for All school in the Bronx in the *New York Times* painted a gloomy portrait.

> *I am to have an S.F.A. group. I receive no training and am given the manual to read. Some teachers learn the system quickly, but for most of us it seems rigid and complex. A staff member dubs it "Stress for All."* . . . *Consultants from S.F.A. make periodic visits to see how we are doing and provide technical help. We are always doing very well by their standards. But as well as we seem to*

> *be doing from the point of view of the S.F.A. organization's staff, that's how badly we are doing according to the Board of Education S.F.A. staff. The principal marches around with an unsmiling S.F.A. coordinator from the board. She is not a happy camper. She stresses that S.F.A. is a business and wants to keep us as clients so it is their job to tell us good things, but the school is not doing well. Teacher morale is low. It could take years to master this program. (Kingon, 2001, pp. 30, 33)*

Once the visitor and principal leave, I sit and watch Ms. Green for about five minutes with Suzanne, and the students are just getting warmed up. I notice how they liven up and laugh with her, responding to her infectious enthusiastic tone; they seem culturally in sync. "Ooooh!" she nearly squeals with delight, her hand resting on her hip while the other waves in the air. "I *like* that answer!" and the student just grins back at her, his face radiant with pride. Watching Ms. Green, I am reminded of a conversation with a close black girlfriend who was in the same teacher education program with me at the university. She described how important it was for her to learn to inhabit both black and white worlds and ways of being if she wanted to be successful in school; I interjected with "code switching" and she replied, "Exactly!" I wonder if that's what I'm observing as the students adjust from white teacher to black teacher. One doesn't seem better than the other, but they are different. Suzanne wrote in an email to me when I asked her about this,

> *She can BE BLACK with them, I can't. It's like when I congratulate them—they all want to do this cool handshake that I just am too WHITE to do with them.*

> *I've noticed that now they compensate and do a regular handshake—they understand that my congrats are different than Ms. Green's. It may not be that I'm too white for some of that—it's just that I'm not comfortable doing it. I don't look cool enough for it, I don't know. But what I find most interesting is when the kids will bring up issues like mean white folks and unfair white people and have these straight discussions with me, as if I'm not white. It's very cool.*

The handshake issue is an example of the socially constructed understandings about what is acceptable and what is not in the classroom, and it's fascinating to me that Suzanne has noted that the different handshake does not detract from the students' ability to have "straight discussions" with her about racism. I can't help wondering if students have picked up on her comfort level and intuitively know what they can and can't do and say, which suggests a very sophisticated kind of respect and understanding of difference. I leave with Suzanne to talk over my notes in the small staff room down the hall.

We begin the meeting in a chatty sort of way and transition into the specific events of the morning. Suzanne listens intently and maintains eye contact, nodding in agreement, but not afraid to interject with questions or comments. When I asked her two weeks later about her recollection of our meeting, she wrote, "First of all, you didn't make me nervous at all when you observed me and I think this is KEY because it allows the teacher to be natural. Secondly, your comments were very specific and that is helpful too. For instance, you noticed when I wished Dashonda happy birthday." The fact that Suzanne used that moment as an example confirmed for me just how important it is to notice such moments. I may be teaching Suzanne, but she is also teaching me.

Student Teaching Problems

Ball and Cohen (1999) argued that the principles and practices of teaching may be taught and learned, and entail three things: inquiry, deliberation on uncertainty in and about practice, and collective debate. Sociocultural perspectives on learning that shift away from individualistic notions of teacher learning have taken hold in certain contexts, building a body of work on practitioner inquiry (Cochran-Smith & Lytle, 2009) and communities of practice (Lave & Wenger, 1991). While these threads run through some teacher education programs, with varying degrees of success in terms of having a long-lasting impact on teacher candidates, there is a sense in the field overall that the rubber meets the road in student teaching, that full-time apprentice teaching will determine readiness to teach on one's own. The classroom immersion is intense and requires student teachers to navigate how theoretical ideas studied in coursework play out in real-life situations. This is mediated by the expectations and norms of the schools hosting the student teachers. In general, the intentionality with respect to coherence between field placements and the principles and practices informing the courses and teacher education program designs leaves much to be desired. In part, this is due to the practical needs of teacher candidates to work in schools within a reasonable geographic vicinity to where they live, and to have placements that both meet certification requirements and match availability of willing partner teachers in those schools. The disconnect felt by Suzanne and some of her peers between the rigidity of their school's Success for All curriculum and the ways they were taught in university coursework to be responsive to students' needs and interests is not at all uncommon in my experience.

In a large-scale review of over a decade of research on teacher preparation and certification, Cochran-Smith and colleagues (2015) discuss the attempts to find solutions to what they describe as a "persistent disconnect between the coursework and fieldwork components of university-based programs" (p. 113). There are promising findings regarding innovative ways to promote peer collaboration and to respond to the intricate complexities and nuances of contextual factors that directly impact what student teachers learn in schools. Yet this review found too that "novice teachers struggle with the reality of schools where policies emphasize student test scores, scripted teaching, and prescribed course content and instructional pacing and where teachers are given little support for collaboration and inquiry" (p. 113). The result is often a disheartening inability to enact needed change as new teachers succumb to the extant school culture. The authors caution that we need to better understand how to address these "divergent views of teaching and learning promoted in universities, on one hand, and those enacted in schools (and increasingly mandated by education policies), on the other hand. Research on successful efforts to disrupt this common outcome is sorely needed" (p. 113).

In an important review of literature on student teaching's contribution to teachers' development in urban and/or high-needs schools, Anderson and Stillman (2013) noted a "cloudy view" both in terms of student teachers' beliefs and attitudes, and in terms of their actual practice. They called for more longitudinal analyses and less reductive views of the role of context and culture in mediating learning. In their own qualitative research on these issues (2011), they identified teacher candidates' opportunities to learn, and the variation in those opportunities, across placements. They also researched how those opportunities served the teachers' need for specialized knowledge once they began full-time teaching in urban, high-needs contexts. Anderson and Stillman (2013) point to the unanswered questions about how thoughts and actions intersect in student teaching, and with what consequences for learning, not just for student teachers, but also for their students.

In many respects, this book is my response to a need to provide an accompanying text for the student teaching experience that gives both practical and theoretical support, beyond overly simplistic survival advice. The five domains explored in the next chapters are interconnected pieces of the work of teaching that in my view are necessary for getting new teachers to experience success and feel confident despite hurdles and setbacks. In my years of supervisory work, I have sought to understand and address the coping mechanisms of student teachers when grappling with dilemmas, especially in cases of tension and dissonance experienced in schools with respect to the philosophies and practices informing the teacher education program and previous coursework. Some important work on these issues was done decades ago when Cochran-Smith analyzed innovations in terms of school-university relations that were rooted in consonance, critical dissonance, and collaborative resonance. She concluded that within preservice teacher education pedagogy there exists "a powerful subtext about teaching and about the boundaries of teacher agency in schools and larger educational systems" (1991, p. 115). Without a means to mediate the dissonance when it occurs, student teachers may simply succumb to the status quo of their school environment, complying with practices and policies even if they clash with their personal beliefs and professional knowledge. The teacher education program, often powerless or unwilling to address these tensions, leaves supervisors and clinical teacher educators with a sort of Russian roulette where the experiences student teachers have in school placements may range from being very conducive to positive learning to requiring triage and damage control.

My advisor in graduate school, Virginia Richardson, is a renowned scholar, with a broad range of research interests that, as she once put it, don't "fit in a box." I recall watching her teach a class and write "best practice" on the board, only to circle and put a slash through it. Her point was beware of those who fail to ask "best for whom?" She was constantly testing assumptions, asking provocative questions, and modeling her own openness to new learning and new perspectives on perennial problems in education. Decades ago, she conducted a study of student teaching and found that discussions at the end of a school day between cooperating teachers and their student teachers focused on classroom management issues rather than more substantive concerns (1988). Strong individualistic norms prevailed in terms of conceptions of teacher learning, and a lack of critical reflection led to inadequate feedback to student teachers. It was also the case that supervisors could not disrupt these norms because of insufficient time to build trust and reciprocity between the demands of the university and the schools. "Effective supervision," she wrote, "must take place, however, within a context that rewards reflection and critical analysis of teaching and has broken the 'independence' norms" (p.

33). Her views on classroom management as much more than rules and routines, but part of how a teacher instructs and models exemplary conduct within a community of learners, and her expertise in how teachers change in their beliefs and practices, have had an immeasurable influence on me. "The description of the teacher that I prefer is one that balances autonomy with community" she wrote. "The teacher is an inquirer, working within a community of practice in which fellow teachers engage, with each other, in critical discussion concerning aims, goals, procedures, and practices" (1998, p. 4). Supporting my student teachers to think and work together in this way, against the strong individualistic norms that still prevail, has been one of the central goals of my teaching.

Reflection and the Five Domains

Poverty, violence, abuse, transience, crime—these are words that often come to mind when imagining the challenges faced by teachers working in urban schools. The teachers I have encountered work hard to overcome these obstacles to their students' learning, and most manage to let hope overshadow despair. In addition to the complexities of understanding their students' often difficult lives, these teachers have to contend with sometimes indifferent or hostile administrators, lack of resources, stressful high-stakes testing, and frequent changes in mandated curriculum.

Yet these teachers maintain a remarkable curiosity about the students in their care. They wonder about them all the time. How do the book choices of girls and boys compare? What happens to spatial reasoning skills when I allow students to explore fractional relationships on a geoboard? How do students play in the block corner, and how does this help them understand their world? Although they may not think of these questions as researchable, many of them are. In fact, some would argue that teaching is inherently a form of qualitative research. Eleanor Duckworth, for example, sees teaching as research because it entails "engaging learners in phenomena and working to understand the sense they are making" (1987, p. 140). Cynthia Ballenger is a teacher researcher who casts her gaze on children who are often marginalized and not well understood, guided by the belief that "the child is always making sense" (2009, p. 6). I too believe that teachers should have a combination of profound respect for and curiosity about children and their ways of coming to understand themselves and their place in the world.

Learning to develop a vision of practice that helps beginning teachers move beyond the more mundane conventions of schooling entails reflective habits of mind (Zeichner & Liston, 1996). In an analysis of her graduate students' writing about dilemmas they faced in their classrooms, Richert asserts that it is the complexity and uncertainty about human relationships that "requires teachers to draw on different and often conflicting values, goals, and commitments as they determine how to act" (2012, p. 7). Cohen (2011) writes that a central predicament teachers face is they are dependent on the cooperation of students, and must learn to unravel the complexity of students' thinking, which adds to the uncertainty of their practice. Ginott (1972) attributes the inherent uncertainty teachers face to the personal relationship between teacher and student.

> *A teacher's response has crucial consequences. It creates a climate of compliance or defiance, a mood of contentment*

> *or contention, a desire to make amends or to take revenge. It affects the child's conduct and character for better or for worse. (p. 38)*

In order to be good at the work of teaching, I have found new teachers require help to develop the ability to step back and to look for patterns in human interactions that facilitate meaningful growth. In doing so, they can more effectively grapple with improvements and changes to practices and routines that are not serving all students well.

Beginning teachers also need reassurance on the value of learning through trial and error. Reflective practice has become a common term in teacher preparation, and pre-service teachers are often told to reflect in a journal-like way in coursework. Reflection on one's own practice is important, but so is having a means to process practices beginning teachers are keenly observing in their field placements. Informal experiences can potentially have an even greater impact on student teachers than their formal teacher education (Feiman-Nemser, 1983). The reflective habit of mind is further developed when written reflections are shared and discussed with others to enhance the social dimensions of learning. Without a clear sense of the value of such writing and discussion, once they leave their teacher preparation programs, new teachers may fall out of the habit of reflecting.

My previous research (Miletta, 2010) examined how the design and implementation of their own practitioner research projects in urban elementary classrooms was educative for beginning teachers. My meta-analyses looked in particular at changes in teachers' beliefs and attitudes that I found were beneficial to stakeholders. I found the year-long projects constituted a transformative learning experience that shaped teachers' beliefs as they learned

- to understand teaching itself as a form of inquiry,
- to see their own potential to produce local funds of knowledge,
- to appreciate a new identity as teacher researcher,
- to feel empowered to defend their teaching decisions, and
- to overcome the boredom and despair of endless mandatory test preparation in the context of education policies.

Despite my findings that research helped cultivate teachers' resiliency and efficacy, there were important realizations about the research studies and interventions, and the teachers' own limitations, in effecting positive change. As a result, I learned to become a better guide for my students, to help them focus on those spaces and places over which they exert control and to use their agency within those areas without fearing accusations of insubordination.

The research stories my student teachers write and share with each other weekly over the course of their student teaching experiences are a different vehicle from an elaborate research project conducted over the course of a year. They follow the same inquiry-based structure of describing, analyzing, and interpreting classroom life, but are short investigations that lend themselves to our group discussions. Sample excerpts will provide a window into how management concerns intersect with the five domains of the work of teaching we will be exploring in the coming chapters. For example, here is a description from Eliza's reflection on a lesson she taught in her pre-K classroom.

> *There was a specific lesson in which the students in my classroom decided to read about earthworms. I read the book aloud, and then we went to the playground. I encouraged them to use sticks to dig, as worms live under the ground. We found one and brought him inside with a leaf, some soil, and a twig in a cup. We watched him move around and lifted the cup to our eyes. It was then that we realized the "worm" had tiny, almost invisible legs, so it couldn't have been a worm at all! We did research and found that some caterpillars look like worms. For three days after this lesson the students went digging for worms and were curious about our caterpillar in the cup, which we had set free.*

It is obvious that this reflection excerpt relates to the domain of planning, and we see how Eliza was able to take cues from her students and follow their growing interest in earthworms. It also relates to the domain of knowing her students, their collective interest in the topic, and their need to go outside and look for worms, and to know more after careful observation of the critter they brought inside in a cup. Her own keen observation skills enabled her to promote her students' knowledge of the subject matter and further develop their intellectual curiosity about the natural world.

It is often the case that the early reflections written by student teachers tell stories about their fears, difficulties, and uncertainties about the responsibilities of teaching students, even in small groups. For example, here is an excerpt from

Adrienne's lesson in a fourth- and fifth-grade special education classroom.

> *The teacher on the second day gave me the fourth graders on my own to teach them test prep strategies in reading. I felt lost but good that I will be able to teach them something I learned when I was young, since I was a struggling reader. But one of my students out of three did not want to participate. I even had to ask him why and try to redirect him to continue on. . . . It was so bad that even the teacher and volunteer came and tried to talk to him, but nothing worked. She had me take the other two fourth graders to another section of the room and finish teaching them. At the end of the day he did the work by himself and had his head down without ever looking at my direction for anything. I tried to reach out to him the next day but nothing.*
>
> *I learned from my supervisor that his mother was dying and that he is traveling far every day to come to school there. The mother feels happy that her children are cared for and loved at this school. This information is very touching, but also let me see what is happening to him outside of school and why he does not want the school to have a spring break. I will try to reach him as well as read his IEP when I get back to work on Wednesday.*

Adrienne writes of her inability to know what to do when faced with a stubborn student who was refusing to participate in the lesson. As she learns of tragedy in his home life, she begins to work on solving the puzzle of how to reach him, and to dig deeper into his learning needs so as to more effectively work with him in the future. Writing and reflecting on moments such as these can enable a teacher to figure out what to do next time a similar situation occurs, and helps avoid jumping to conclusions based on initial impressions. As teachers learn from their students by uncovering what they know, think, and can do, they're learning about their teaching too.

Early reflections also explore what student teachers learn about planning when things don't go as planned. Elisabeth wrote about learning to practice reading aloud before teaching.

> *My first day of doing a read aloud was difficult. I could not get all of the children to listen and stay on task. I must say that it was a very humbling experience. I thought to myself, "What can I do to get these kids interested?" I practiced and practiced reading the book for the next read aloud. The next day went much better and each day since then has been a success. Practice makes perfect! I even was asked to reread a great book,* Peter's Chair, *over since the children enjoyed the reading so much. We discussed the characters in the book and the setting. We also went over what makes a great retelling. . . . I plan to focus on being more self-aware of my approach and how the students respond to different positive behaviors that I display. Going home and reflecting on the day's events is a learning experience.*

Elisabeth contrasts the first unsuccessful read aloud with the subsequent two in terms of student enjoyment and engagement, and her ability to debrief criteria for summarizing the story. She also sets a personal goal to build her self-awareness and continue to reflect on each day's teaching.

Similarly, Miranda noted that rushing and feeling uncertain about the pacing of her lesson was unsettling for her, and the students became restless.

> *I know that I have to know it is okay to modify a lesson and take some things out if necessary. I didn't do this because I felt since I was being observed . . . I had to do absolutely everything in the lesson, even if it meant taking out the students' time discussing and working together. I know to take a deep breath and move at the pace of the class, because I'm there to teach them and make sure they retain what I teach. I know all the things to do right, but I became flustered and nervous and forgot to do those things. I now know that it's okay to stop for a moment and assess what the class reaction is; if what I'm doing and the pace I am moving at is not okay, then I have to change tactics and know this is okay.*

It's not a coincidence that Miranda uses the words "know" and "okay" so much in this reflection; it's clear that she is reinforcing her own personal realization that deviating from a lesson plan is normal and necessary, and that taking cues from students will help her in the future with pacing.

As student teachers become more acclimated to the classroom and are getting to know their students, they begin to explore the domain of collaboration more in their reflections. Eve was in her second placement in a fifth-grade ICT classroom that was team taught, and also had a teacher aide in the room to work one-on-one with a special-needs student. She reflected on how an unexpected tragedy disrupted the normalcy of her classroom and required the teachers to collectively address how the event was affecting the students.

Today was the first day back from a long weekend and the mood this morning was somber. It wasn't for the reason that you may think; with the sound of helicopters flying overhead, we decided to start the day talking about the crash. The Metro North crash that occurred on Sunday morning happened in the neighborhood where our school is located. Many of the children in my class have apartments overlooking the Spuyten Duyvil train station. We gave each of the children who wanted to talk about it a chance to speak. Some of the children who lived in the apartment buildings spoke about being able to see the crash off their balconies. Others spoke about returning home from being away for Thanksgiving and it taking hours to get back into their apartments. Some children from the class went with their parents to see all of the news crews and helicopters. Children also spoke about their concerns that if it had been this morning that many of their parents could have been on that exact train. Some spoke of taking the Metro North on the weekends with their families to go to the city and that it could have been them. We were all feeling a deep sense of sadness for all those who lost their lives and everyone else who was injured or affected by this tragedy. It was a topic of discussion that was unavoidable, and we as teachers needed to address it. We reflected on our feelings, and the sound of helicopters overhead all day was a constant reminder that life can be cut short and to cherish every moment.

This is a dramatic example, but there are often cases when normalcy is disrupted and teachers must grapple with helping students cope, while shielding them from undue graphic violence or horror. Bringing the classroom community together for an appropriate sharing of their reactions, fears, and hopes requires collective sensitivity and skill.

Rita taught in a preschool and wrote about a discussion among colleagues at their monthly meeting about how they were responding to students' behavior.

> *Last Thursday, as I sat with my fellow teachers during our monthly teacher meeting, we discussed the importance of acknowledging children's positive behaviors. As we moved forward to describe a moment or a behavior in our classrooms, it became evident how many negative statements a child receives during a day. At some point in our busy classrooms we will inadvertently say to a child: Don't run! Stop talking! You don't listen, etc., or we will hear a child tell another you are ugly or I don't like you.*
>
> *Children need to feel that we appreciate them. Praise encourages them to perform more efficiently and assess their strengths. Nevertheless, if you give a child praise without a constructive meaning, you are creating an individual who will become a* pleaser *instead of a self-motivated individual who values his/her own voice. Therefore, effective praise takes the form of positive feedback. It focuses on the child's own sense of accomplishment.*

Rita has taken away from this interaction with other teachers that it is easy to lose awareness of the types of comments made to students throughout the day. Undue negativity can not only harm individual children; it can cause them to be unkind with each other. Praise without substance can have the unintended consequence of making children seek to please adults without developing their own sense of self-worth. Reflecting on this conversation gave Rita an opportunity to articulate an important understanding. In a subsequent reflection about a different event, Rita wrote about becoming more attuned to the kind of teacher she wanted to be.

> *I picked this moment because it made me think about who I want to be as a teacher, how I should treat my students, and how I expect them to treat me. Certainly, I want them to remember how much I care for them. I want them to remember the times I listened about their fears, their dreams, and their hopes. I want them to remember even though I will make mistakes, and they will make mistakes, we will learn together from those mistakes and move on. I want them to know that I will push them hard because I have faith that they all can achieve great things. Finally, I want to provide them a structured environment where they can become dynamic individuals.*

There is something about narrowing the focus in these reflections to a moment, to an important and memorable event, that leads to being able to be more self-critical, to unravel the meaning of what occurred, and to draw an implication that is both personal and universal. Sharing and talking about these moments and events amplify these outcomes, and create meaningful bonds of understanding among teachers, making them feel less alone.

Walk the Talk

As a teacher educator, I spend a lot of time thinking about and talking about teaching. I choose to supervise student teachers and visit lots of different schools, because it helps me to see ideas in action, and it makes me a better teacher, both for my college students and for young people when I have opportunities to interact with them in classrooms. These actions and reflections naturally also intersect with concerns about learning, as I talk with my graduate students about their learning and the learning of their students in schools. I find I am often asking them to imagine what certain experiences are like for the learners in their charge, just as I try to imagine what it is like for them to be learning about the remarkable early childhood schools of Reggio Emilia in Italy, or Patricia Carini's Descriptive Review of the Child in my courses. Sometimes I am reminded too through my own personal experiences of learning just how difficult and uncomfortable it can be, and this often takes me back to thinking about the role of the teacher.

For example, a few years ago I had an opportunity to study voice with a professional actor who has performed lead roles in Broadway musicals. I stopped taking private music lessons back in college, and aside from a few lessons on vocal technique a decade ago, I have not formally studied voice. I am more of a flutist by training, but I love to sing and have had experiences with lots of different kinds of vocal music. My teacher is highly respected as a voice teacher, so when she agreed to take me on as a student for a few weeks between other commitments, I felt an explosion of emotions: dread, excitement, insecurity, elation. Learning to sing well is really hard work. It is physically demanding, requiring lung power and muscular flexibility, but it is also mentally draining. Extreme focus and concentration are required, not to mention memorization of words, notes, and phrases. I understood my teacher's instructions by doing and feeling the mind-body connection that makes singing possible. It's a tremendous act of faith, to sing: you have to believe that if you concentrate and focus your mind enough, your body will respond and the desired sounds will result from those efforts. Listening and striving to emulate what is heard are absolutely essential for promoting understanding. But all that hard work pays off in noticeable results. The gratification of feeling that you nailed it makes all the hard work worth it.

Being a learner has also heightened my awareness of other things that good teachers must do for their students. Learning can be hard, even terrifying, but it can also be fun. My voice lessons were filled with moments of shared laughter. We often paused to share a little story or remember a previous experience. My teacher has a wicked sense of humor, and I found that laughing helped me to be more relaxed, which is absolutely essential to produce a quality vocal sound. It also helps me to not take myself too seriously, and greatly reduces my fear of performing badly. All good teachers know the importance of having high expectations of their students. My voice teacher knew that I have a full-time career and no plans to go public with my singing any-time soon. But she still kept me from treating the lessons as a pastime or hobby with the expectation that I would be as professional about our work together as her professional students. This made me say to myself, well, I better practice! While my teacher sometimes suggested songs for me to work on and practice, she also gave me plenty of choices. The freedom afforded me was immensely motivating and has given me an ever-expanding possible repertoire to draw on. I find myself listening to music now more attentively, considering the many possible options available to me as

I think to myself, could I sing that? How might I begin to work on that?

Learning requires hard work, faith, fun, and high expectations, and learners are motivated when they have choice and freedom. Keep this list growing as you think about your own experiences as a learner. How did you learn to take apart a bicycle and put it back together again? Or to make your mother's beef stew taste as good as hers? When you think back on memorable teachers and the learning opportunities afforded you, what strikes you as important? How might revisiting your own learning experiences in the past help you to think about the kind of teacher you'd like to be? You want to teach with integrity, to be yourself as much as possible. Van Manen wrote that "we need to be aware how we, as teachers, are known by our children as we are captured in turn by their glance" (1986, p. 49). See, and be seen. That is how you can work on walking the talk and improving the practice of teaching.

Chapter 2

Planning

Plan for Success

In *Teacher* (1963) New Zealand writer Sylvia Ashton-Warner provides us with a detailed portrait of her classroom with stories that can be funny, wild, touching, and provocative. The mix of Maori and white students of European descent in her care have made her wisdom a bedrock for our increasingly diverse, multicultural world inside schools.

> *For every work, and first of all that of a teacher, must have its form, its design. And the design of my work is that creativity in this time of life when character can be influenced forever is the solution to the problem of war. To me it has the validity of a law of physics and all the unstatable, irrepressible emotion of beauty. (p. 100)*

Words to live by. How does teaching make the world more peaceful? What will be the design of your work?

The ability to improvise and think on your feet can serve you well in a teaching career, but as a rule of thumb it's essential to have a well-thought-out plan ahead of time. Teachers plan in many ways, by making little mental notes, writing things down in a weekly paper planner, or entering information on a digital platform, talking together with other teachers at the same grade level, or who teach specialized subjects, and even while going shopping or commuting to and from school. These plans involve micro details, such as materials needed for a particular activity, and macro ideas about how what is to come is connected to what came before, and everything in between. Therefore, learning to plan is not as simple as some would have you believe. You can't just learn to use a particular lesson plan format, fill it in, and believe that all will go according to the plan. Even experienced teachers have to cope with the unexpected disruptions, fascinating tangents, and miscalculated timing and pacing of activities that occur on a regular basis in any given teaching day.

Call the Parent?

I recall a student teacher during an observation who had to learn a lesson the hard way about taking discipline actions. She had decided to handle misbehavior with a warning, and then a threat to call the parent of the misbehaving student. She quickly ran into the problem of having to save face by calling parents, and decided to do so in the moment. Soon she had so many students lined up as she was dialing numbers of parents that the lesson completely fell apart.

Veteran teachers have a big advantage over novices, however. They have previous experience. The first year of teaching is akin to exploring a vast territory of the unknown. Much of the learning occurs as mistakes are made. Errors of pacing, failing to take children's needs into account, or simply not thinking through unintended consequences of a particular action or punishment strategy are common problems for beginning teachers. Sometimes it can feel quite painful. These types of experiences can be demoralizing and erode a new teacher's fragile self-confidence. But there is no escaping the fact that especially for beginning teachers, there are two parallel and paradoxical tasks: teach, and learn to teach as you are teaching.

The methods courses that are designed to prepare teachers for the considerable demands of planning and teaching subject matter often suggest particular formats for lesson plans. These vary not only by subject matter and teaching method, but also by scope (lesson, unit, or year-long plan). Furthermore, different instructors and different institutions will use varying approaches to teaching planning, and these don't always match up with commercially available curriculum and school district expectations. Most importantly, even the most detailed lesson plan, aligned with standards and assessment expectations, usually leaves out the all-important question of context. In other words, the lesson must be designed for particular students, in a particular context, and include considerations of what learning has preceded the experience and what will follow. This is why a teacher following a supposedly foolproof script may experience total disaster in the classroom if little or no attention is paid to context.

LESSON PLANNING 101

In an effort to simplify the process of learning about lesson planning for the beginning preservice teachers I have taught, I devised a four-part framework that is structured around these essential questions:

1. What do I want to teach?
2. Why does it matter?
3. How will I teach?
4. How will I know what students learned?

Another way to think about these questions is:

Curriculum = What I want to teach

Rationale = Why it matters

Instruction = How I will teach

Assessment = How I will know what students learned

It's worth spending time to consider some aspects of each of these before continuing with other details of the planning framework.

Curriculum

Curriculum can mean many things, and its definition is ever-changing. Some think of the curriculum in terms of how subject matter is broken down into categories such as language arts, mathematics, science, social studies, and so on. Hilda Taba, a scholar of social studies in the 1960s, said that curriculum was simply a plan for learning (1962). Others have broadened its meaning to notions of a life course and paths of action (Clandinin & Connelly, 1988). A famous educational philosopher, Maxine Greene, equated curriculum with possibility:

> *Students must be enabled, at whatever stages they find themselves to be, to encounter curriculum as possibility. By that I mean curriculum ought to provide a series of occasions for individuals to articulate the themes of their existence and to reflect on those themes until they know themselves to be in the world and can name what has been up to then obscure.* (1978, pp. 18–19)

Curriculum does not exist in some abstract vacuum, but must be enacted with real students, in a particular context. Joseph Schwab wrote, "The curriculum constructed of these

"I'll tell you the secret to good teaching: make possible an experience without predetermining what that experience will be." —Maxine Greene

particulars will be brought to bear, not in some archetypical classroom, but in a particular locus in time and space with smells, shadows, seats, and conditions outside its walls which may have much to do with what is achieved inside" (1978, pp. 309–310). Curriculum, then, is sometimes a bit intangible and unpredictable, even though the way the word is used in schools often suggests a more concrete definition.

One possible reason for the persistent way of thinking about curriculum mostly as something captured in scope and sequence documents, textbooks and teacher guides is that schools are always under a lot of pressure to be accountable for student learning, which is still more often than not measured with inadequate and unsophisticated tests. Despite these constraints and resulting problems, it is still possible for teachers to have some say in what is taught to children. To make wise choices, teachers need to know their students, picking up on clues about special interests, current events, popular culture, favorite authors, and being attuned to what is intrinsically interesting to them. They should also not hesitate to bring their own interests into the classroom; students respond very favorably when they recognize the teacher's enthusiasm for the subject under study.

> The pernicious effects of high-stakes testing are placing more constraints on schools and have led to a narrowing of the curriculum to what is included on the tests.

Rationale

A teacher must be prepared at all times to answer that dreaded question, "Why are we doing this?" We shouldn't have to dread the why-do-I-have-to-do-this issue because presumably we go into teaching thinking that learning is exciting and wonderful. There is no doubt that time spent doing boring drudgery in the classroom will inevitably lead to discipline problems and students seeking an outlet for their creative energy and active imaginations. Answers that shift the burden of responsibility for thinking through the rationale for the curriculum to others, such as "it's in the standards" or "it's what the district requires" won't make the ensuing problems go away. Teachers need to know why they are doing what they are doing, and when they are unsure or don't know, disaster is sure to follow.

Fortunately, there's an endless bounty of interesting and exciting things worth studying. What makes a curriculum's rationale particularly strong? Here are a few features to get you started; no doubt you can add some more. Often

What makes something worth studying? It is

open-ended;
generative;
complex and challenging;
controversial and provocative;
puzzling;
connected to a personal concern or interest;
part of the natural world;
new, fantastic, undiscovered;
socially engaging;
enjoyable and fun; and
a compelling narrative.

____

____

____

When I was in elementary school, we built this geodesic dome, based on the designs of Buckminster Fuller (see www.bfi.org), on the playground. Projects that are interdisciplinary and involve students across grade levels leave a lasting impression.

beginning teachers pick a curriculum without thinking through in every detail whether what they have chosen is really of value to students and their learning. It should be the case that if a visitor were to drop in at any time of the day and ask the teacher the purpose and value of whatever students were doing, there would be a logical and meaningful answer.

The rationale for the curriculum should also take into account the *continuity of experience* that is so important in children's learning. Chopping up big ideas into too many little pieces, or creating a schedule where students jump from activity to activity with no connection to what came the day before or will come the next day does not promote meaningful and long-lasting learning. Continuity of experience also has to do with making in-school learning related to out-of-school learning. Christopher Clark (1990) provides a vivid account of a first-grade teacher's lesson on making applesauce, something that is commonly part of an early childhood curriculum. He points out that among the reasons for doing such an activity with young children, food preparation provides a link between home and school. Furthermore, the first graders had recently been on two field trips, to a cider mill, and to a farmer's market. As he writes, intended learning outcomes from these experiences were "life outside school is (or can be) connected to life in school; that school learning activities need not be segregated from one's taken-for-granted everyday knowledge and learning" (p. 329).

Instruction

Most people think about lesson plans as the description of a sequence of activities and actions that will take place in a classroom learning experience. It is certainly true that a plan for learning must include some notion of what will take place, what materials are necessary and how they will be used, what students and the teacher will be expected to do and say and accomplish in a given time frame, and methods that will be adopted. In order to be successful, the instruction part of a lesson plan should have a thoughtful choice about appropriate method given the curriculum under study. Is it appropriate to lead students in an inquiry if they are learning procedures for a fire drill? Probably not, just as you probably would not want them to explore and experiment with a Bunsen burner if they have never used one before.

The instruction part of the lesson plan must also factor in the most suitable participation structures and delineate decisions about when and how students will work alone, with a partner, in a small group, or as a whole class. The oral, written, and performance-based tasks that students will be asked to work on should also be scaffolded in a sequence that makes sense given the goals of the curriculum. Just as the assessments should account for the process of learning as well as the product of that learning, so too must the instructional plan provide the opportunities for learning in a way that will make the assessments as meaningful as possible.

Veteran kindergarten teacher and author Julie Diamond (2008) says children learn best through concrete experiences. A study of squirrels gave her students opportunities for firsthand observations of real things found in their city environment.

It's also important to keep in mind that the instruction part of a lesson plan is not a fixed prediction of exactly what will occur during the lesson. Teachers have to be prepared to deviate from the plan when there's evidence that students are not understanding something, or when an interesting tangent provides a learning opportunity worth pursuing, or whenever the plan needs adjusting for other reasons. When I was a student teacher, we were required to include a list of outcomes, abbreviated with the acronym, SWBAT (Students Will Be Able To), on all our lesson plans. We quickly learned from experience that this was more of a wish list than a predictable outcome.

Assessment

In my work with beginning teachers, I have noticed that they don't tend to realize that circulating in the classroom to monitor students' work and conversations, or asking for thumbs up or down responses, constitutes "real" assessment. But formative assessment practices that capture the learning process as it is unfolding are just as important as the summative assessments that often lead to cumulative evaluations of students' progress. They also provide crucial clues to the teacher about how the goals and aims for the lesson are being met as the lesson is occurring. All lesson planning must provide for multiple ways of assessing learning that include oral and written tasks, and that can assess individual as well as group learning.

This doesn't mean that every lesson plan must include a scoring rubric that is task specific, or a test, or some writing component in its assessment of the learning. Nor should it be assumed that all assessment is completed by students and evaluated by the teacher afterward. Students can do self-assessment, and should evaluate the quality of their own work at times and self-assess their progress with particular projects, topics, and their stated personal goals. Teachers can make notes and provide feedback in one-on-one conferences or as they circulate and listen to students at work. Varying the methods of assessing learning makes for a more dynamic interchange between and among students and the teacher, and ensures that being evaluated isn't a dreaded and hated part of learning. Students should be made to feel proud of their accomplishments, and eager to share their learning with their peers and teacher in ways that don't threaten their sense of self-esteem or personal pride.

Finally, assessments must be designed with provisions in mind for those students with Individual Education Plans (IEPs) or other kinds of special needs. This is also why context is so crucial, and why it is important to know your students well when designing assessments. Vito Perrone wrote an account of his experience with a student who made it to high school without basic skills in literacy and little desire to read and write. Instead of continuing to fail the student, as others had likely done, he provided opportunities for this student to prepare oral presentations on a variety of interesting topics including rockets, pyramids, and how telephones work. "He established for me a basis for ongoing conversation with him that was rooted in real content—even though it was not always related to what we were studying at the time." The student benefited, further developing his literacy skills, and the class learned some interesting content as well as to think in new ways about difference. Perrone also "was forced to reflect more seriously about what constitutes learning and how it is to be assessed" (2000, p. 13).

Putting It All Together

Addressing these four components of a lesson plan by making decisions pertaining to *curriculum*, its *rationale*, the *instructional plan*, and *assessments* can be done in a variety of formats. Choices about what is the most appropriate format will depend on the purpose of the lesson, personal preferences for making and using plans, and the audience for the plan. Although the questions are useful to keep in mind when planning mentally, it's always helpful to get those mental notes down on paper (or better yet, into a digital form that can be saved and retrieved). It's easy as a beginning teacher to get into the habit of writing plans in shorthand and on scraps of paper, and then wishing the following year that there was a more permanent record of the plan and how it was enacted. When writing a plan to be shared with a principal, a colleague, a coach, or a professor, including details in clear, concise language is essential. Often the teachers I have worked with write a full narrative they develop from notes and bullet points when they are preparing lessons for a course assignment. Although the narrative is not necessarily divided into four discrete sections, as there is some overlap between the curriculum and its rationale, and the instruction and assessments, all questions are addressed. Let's look at the breakdown of subquestions for each of the four parts.

Curriculum

What do I want to teach?

What particular skills, knowledge, understanding, and/or beliefs are the focus of this learning experience?

(*continued*)

Which learning experiences are most important for these students within the context of knowing and representing this particular subject matter?

Thinking about the curricular choices entails not only selecting the piece of content or subject matter that will be explored, but also a consideration of weighing the benefits and drawbacks of selecting certain kinds of learning experiences and discarding others. To some extent, scope and sequence documents, teacher guides and standards will help make broad-stroke decisions about appropriate content choices for grade levels. But just because studying world geography is traditionally an upper elementary grade level subject, that doesn't mean first graders won't be interested in knowing more about Africa, or which countries are in Europe and where you can find them on a map. Similarly, while young children often study their surrounding community, older students may become interested in community activism and organizing, and can participate in service learning projects that entail in-depth knowledge about their local community.

Rationale

Why does it matter?

Why are the concepts, materials, methods of inquiry, and activities worth spending time on in this subject matter?

In what ways does the lesson connect to the lives of these students?

What aspects of this lesson will actively engage them and their curiosity?

Thinking through the rationale for the chosen curriculum is more complex than it seems at first. Not only is it important to articulate why the curricular choices are worthwhile pursuits for classroom study in and of themselves, teachers have to also be cognizant of how those topics and activities will connect to the interests of the specific children in question. Vivian Paley is an example of a teacher and writer who has spent a lifetime writing about how listening to her students enabled her to pursue with them such intrinsically meaningful topics as friendship, fairness, and fantasy play, with additional excursions into investigations of the natural world. In general terms, her years of experience with 5-year-olds helped her to know that such topics would interest them, but she nevertheless had to listen to and observe particular children to figure out the clues in their conversation, behavior, and play that would illuminate the things that would provide a point of departure for her curricular decisions. Knowing what will be interesting to your students based on evidence you have gathered will go a long way toward guaranteeing the success of the lessons you want to teach.

Instruction

How will I teach it?

What methods, materials, routines, and task structures will be used in this lesson, and when and how will students work alone, in pairs, or in small groups?

What is the sequence of activities, and what are the roles of the teacher and of the students for each?

How does this particular lesson fit into the overall goals for this unit, and how will I make that explicit for students?

(*continued*)

What precedes and will follow this lesson, and how will students be helped to make those connections?

What accommodations are necessary for students with special needs?

How might this lesson promote a fair and equitable classroom climate in which mutual respect among all class members is fostered?

The nuts and bolts of a lesson plan are found in the instructional decisions that entail figuring out what students will be doing, how they will engage in the learning experiences, and what is the best sequence for those experiences. Some types of instructional decisions become familiar routines, like a morning problem to work on as students arrive at school, or a workshop time when students are engaged in ongoing projects. But the expectations for what students should be doing, why it matters, and how to do it must be clear or discipline problems and misbehavior are bound to occur. Teachers also need to think through how they are accommodating students with special needs or helping those who have been absent to catch up with other students. Finally, all instructional decisions should also take into account moral dimensions of teaching in the interests of continuing to build a classroom climate that is grounded in principles of trust and respect, and that helps students learn to treat each other fairly and equitably.

Assessment

How will I know what students learned?

What are ways to check for understanding during the lesson?

What formative and summative assessments will be used?

How will provisions be made for those who either missed the lesson or still need additional help?

How will students articulate their learning for each other?

The assessment decisions teachers make are intricately connected to instructional decisions because as teachers plan a sequence of learning activities, they also need to plan for ways to know the extent to which those activities were successful in meeting desired goals. In a memorable documentary made at Harvard University's Smithsonian Center for Astrophysics titled *A Private Universe* (1987, https://www.learner.org/series/a-private-universe), a ninth-grade science class is the focus of the filmmakers' attempts to examine where people's basic understandings about the orbits of the sun, moon, and earth go awry. Many people explain the reasons for seasonal weather changes as the result of the earth being closer or farther from the sun, even though the earth's orbit is nearly circular and the tilt of the earth's axis with respect to its orbital plane is the important concept to understand. A bright student named Heather, who has been doing well on classroom assessments, on closer investigation reveals bizarre theories and misconceptions, including a belief that the earth's orbit around the sun is a "curlicue" shape. The filmmakers provide a vivid wake-up call to educators to pay

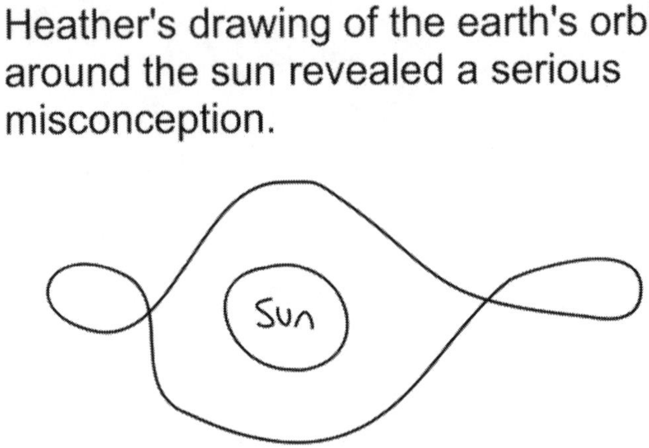

close attention to students' understandings. The more robust the ways that teachers can check for understanding as lessons unfold, the greater the likelihood that students will do well on summative assessments and will be successful in articulating their learning for others.

In addition to these four parts of the framework, there are some questions below that are also useful to keep in mind when planning lessons. These are particularly important in terms of avoiding and preventing discipline problems. Involving students as much as possible will ensure their active engagement during the lesson. Even if there are already assigned classroom jobs for tasks such as helping to distribute materials, cleaning up, or inspecting the work areas, try to include students in as many ways as possible. Be clear about what students need to do once they finish a task and where their work needs to go. Think ahead of time about your ability to handle a disruption during the lesson, and when possible, have other adults helping out so that you can step out for a moment to privately confer with a student or to help settle a conflict.

Additional Considerations

How much time has been allotted for each part of the lesson, and what are the contingency plans if the pacing gets off track?

What are appropriate levels of noise and movement given the tasks at hand, and have those been effectively communicated to students?

How can students be involved in helping during the lesson (i.e., with distributing materials, cleaning up, checking their work, etc.)?

What will happen if there's a discipline problem during the lesson?

How might additional adults be helpful (student teachers, aides, parents, etc.)?

While careful and thoughtful planning of lessons that incorporates specific students' interests, questions, and needs and takes contextual factors into account can go a long way to assuring a reduction of discipline and management problems in the classroom, there may still be circumstances and situations in which they occur. Therefore, it is important to communicate with students not only about the norms and expectations for their participation but also the consequences for unacceptable behavior. I always prefer to follow up an incident with a private conversation, and if other students or adults were involved or potentially harmed, then the consequences usually entail verbal or written apologies and actions to correct the harm. Punishments and threats that may seem arbitrary to students will most certainly disrupt the flow of the lesson and can derail progress made toward a harmonious and healthy classroom climate. It's

> Public humiliation and other forms of harsh punishments may seem effective when trying to be strict about boundaries and limits, but in the long run they backfire. Don't damage your relationships with students by making this mistake; it's not easily repaired.

also important to collectively reflect on what's working and to make time for students to discuss possible alternatives, or ways that certain routines might be improved, or what they will do differently in the future.

LESSON PLANNING IN STUDENT TEACHING

Institutions with teacher preparation programs have traditionally spent a great deal of time on lesson planning. In the not-so-distant-past, teachers were largely responsible for many aspects of planning across the continuum, from micro details such as the grouping of students, to more macro notions such as mapping units of study through the academic year. Nowadays, with an increased focus on accountability and standards, most teachers are expected to use curriculum guides and prepared materials, as well as follow their district's guidelines for covering content and meeting standards. As a result of the increased focus on student learning and measuring achievement, student teachers are also being asked to do more in-depth analysis of their teaching. With only a limited number of meetings between student teachers, their supervisors, and their cooperating teachers, it's important to make the most of these learning opportunities, as it's likely to be the time in the first years of a person's teaching career in which the most support and guidance is provided.

The requirements for becoming certified as a teacher are also undergoing changes. Many policies for certification are requiring multiple standardized exams, including teacher performance assessments that include video and analysis of teaching. Some programs also use a hybrid model of in-person observations and analysis of videotaped lessons. It's one thing to discuss a lesson with a supervisor on site following an observation, and quite another to analyze a videotape with in-depth commentary to be submitted for evaluation, feedback, and scoring.

In my own teaching, I had always asked my students to submit to me and their cooperating teacher(s) a pre-observation memo together with their lesson plan prior to an observation. It was divided into four parts:

1. Planning, Preparation for Learning, and Delivery of Instruction

    - Briefly describe your lesson and what you hope students will learn from this lesson, with a focus on particular skills, knowledge, understanding, and/or beliefs. Provide any necessary context (what came before, prior knowledge of students, etc.).
    - How is this learning important within the context of the subject matter? Why are the concepts, materials, methods of inquiry, and activities worth spending time on?
    - How will your lesson actively engage your students and enable them to construct meaning?

2. Classroom Management and Learning Environment
    - How might this lesson promote a climate in which learning is valued, fair and equitable standards for conduct are upheld, and mutual respect among all class members is fostered?
3. Assessment
    - How will you know your students have learned what you intended?
4. Professional Growth and Development
    - Briefly describe the particular skills or areas of your teaching you would like us to focus on during this observation.

I find that framing questions in this way facilitates my students' learning and helps them to make connections to my four-part framework and other lesson plan formats they are accustomed to using. The memos also help in our post-observation conversations as we go over my notes and compare the plan to what actually transpired. We usually spread out the students' work and have a look together to share initial impressions, talk about specific students, and begin to identify patterns. Sometimes there is also a post-observation memo that helps my students to think about something they want to explore in more depth in a weekly reflection.

How does this all come together in a real example from one of my student teachers? Jennifer was placed in a fifth-grade Integrated Co-Teaching (ICT) classroom with two cooperating teachers, and for her first observation she taught a lesson to a small group about the Jacob Lawrence picture book *The Great Migration* (1995) adapted from ReadyGen curriculum published by Pearson in 2014. All of the students were experiencing difficulties with reading, and four had Individualized Education Plans (IEPs). Their learning disabilities meant that she would have to provide targeted instruction in reading strategies. In her pre-observation memo she wrote, "I have chosen self-monitoring for this lesson because it is an important reading strategy that students can learn and practice on their own. . . . In this lesson, students will read the second half of *The Great Migration* as a group and in pairs. Working in pairs, students will practice using self-monitoring with graphic organizers to record their thoughts. Students will later reflect on their self-monitoring notes in a group discussion." In the first section of the memo, Jennifer wrote about a student in the group:

> *One student of concern is Angie. She has missed over twenty days of school as of this writing and it is beginning to show in her academic performance. Angie is also extremely shy and has difficulty vocalizing when she doesn't understand something or needs additional help, even when she is asked directly by a teacher. I hope that this lesson engages Angie and helps her develop self-monitoring as one of her reading strategies, but will definitely be focusing additional attention on her to see if my instructional choices need to be modified in the future.*

She also provided details on the students' IEPs and recent reading assessments.

Jennifer's lesson plan was very detailed. For example, in the Launch or Hook section of the plan she wrote the following:

I will tell students that today they will finish reading The Great Migration *to find out what happened to the migrants once they arrived in the North.*

I will tell students that a good way to make sure they are understanding what they are reading so that they can write about it later is to self-monitor. I will ask for a volunteer to tell the group what it means to self-monitor.

I will tell students that self-monitoring is being aware of what you are reading. I will tell students they will self-monitor when they stop and make a prediction about what will happen next or when they stop and realize they are confused about something. I will ask students if this has ever happened while they are reading and allow them to give some examples.

I will explain that sometimes you may realize that you don't understand what you are reading or that you are unclear about the meaning of a word. I will tell students that today they will use sticky notes to practice self-monitoring as they read. I will make sure they understand that with enough practice, eventually they will be able to self-monitor without the sticky notes. This activity is meant to help them make it a habit as they read.

I will give students a choice of which graphic organizer they would like to use for this activity.

I will ask students to formulate predictions about what they think will happen to the migrants in the second half of the book. I will call on volunteers to share with the group.

None of this was explicitly spelled out in the teacher's guide of the curriculum. Jennifer had decided that explicit work on self-monitoring using sticky notes would enable students to strengthen this skill necessary for their growth as readers. Unlike the teacher's guide, which had specific questions and answers spelled out, for example regarding the vocabulary "quarters" on page 37 in the text, Jennifer provided a few open-ended examples of when and how they might use a sticky note:

> *I will stop at the end of page 27 and ask students, "What does the 'black press' mean?" Tell them that if they were unsure, this was something they would write on a sticky note and put on the page.*
>
> *I will stop at the end of page 34 and ask students, "Why might the agents have been able to avoid arrest just by wearing a disguise?" I will tell them that if they were unsure, this was something they would write on a sticky note and put on the page.*
>
> *I will ask students to turn to their neighbor and finish reading the book together in pairs. I will tell students that as they are reading, they should mark pages with sticky notes to practice self-monitoring. I will tell students that at the end of the lesson, they will stick their notes onto the self-monitoring strategies worksheet and I will be collecting them.*
>
> *When students have finished reading with a partner, I will ask for volunteers to share their self-monitoring notes with the group. I will ask for volunteers to discuss any misconceptions that students had and be sure that all misconceptions are resolved.*

Jennifer also noted in the Academic Language section of her plan the vocabulary that she needed to focus on in the lesson: migration, industrial, quarters, segregation, disdain, storefront church, and calloused. When discussing disdain, one student remarked, "They didn't treat them good." Jennifer helped them to notice how context clues were helpful in figuring out meanings, and when another student wondered about segregation in the north, Jennifer commented that wondering as you read is a good thing that all readers do. On page 60 in the text, they discussed the word "triumphs" as compared to "struggles" and then Kendra wondered aloud that since white people had more power, couldn't they just take the jobs? Jennifer explained that there was so much racism at the time that blacks and whites had widely different earnings, and those who cost less got work.

In writing up a post-observation memo, Jennifer noted that students understood the self-monitoring strategy and "that some of the students made some interesting connections to the text during the discussion portion of the lesson. This gave me evidence that their stopping to interact with the text through self-monitoring increased their reading comprehension." Five days later, in a reflection she wrote about the moment when Kendra wondered about why white people didn't take jobs if they had more power:

> *One student, Kendra, raised her hand and said she wondered about the part in the book that talks about white people and black people fighting over jobs in the north. "Hmm," I said to the group. "What do we think? Why would they be fighting?" Kendra raised her hand again and said, "If the whites had more power, why wouldn't they just take the jobs?" I was blown away. Of course, she was right. I had one of those moments where about ten things ran through my head that I could have said in response. I decided to take the discussion in the direc-*

tion of "the northern business owners were hiring the migrants because they were able to do so more cheaply" and that was that. Later I knelt down by her desk and said, "I was very impressed with your comments today during the discussion. I can tell you really think about what you're reading." She beamed at me.

This moment showed me something important. Kendra has been diagnosed with ADHD and has related behavioral issues. She is disruptive. She talks over the teachers and sometimes can barely stay in her seat. However, when we are doing work with reading and discussion in response to reading, she will usually have one or two insightful comments that seem to save the discussion from getting a little too tedious or repetitive. I reflected later on just how much Kendra surprised me in our discussion. I've eavesdropped on many special education teachers talking about their students in terms of what they can't do. Really, it should be the opposite. Why not focus on what they can do and play to those strengths?

I think it's easy as a teacher, even when you have the best of intentions, to make assumptions about what students are capable of and what they already know. Kendra is an insightful thinker and an excellent reader, despite the label of her diagnosis that she has to carry around with her. Sometimes her behavior can obscure her talents as a student. It's my job as a teacher to always remember that those talents are there.

I think this example shows the complexities of learning to plan with specific children in mind. Jennifer's epiphany on being surprised by Kendra's contribution to the discussion, and her ability to apply the strategy of self-monitoring, wondering aloud about an important aspect of the historical period in which *The Great Migration* occurred, illustrate that simply learning to follow the teaching guide is insufficient for successful teaching. Jennifer's reflection also shows her ability to learn both from and with her students, and to appreciate that Kendra's contributions and talents keep discussions from being "too tedious or repetitive" and that there is so much more to her than the ADHD label and disruptive behavior.

We'll continue to think about how classroom management is related to planning in the next chapter on reflection, and in chapter 5 on working with colleagues, for much planning is done in tandem with other teachers. In chapter 4, we'll explore how planning for the start of the school year and getting to know your students in the first weeks of school are also related to connections between classroom management and planning. The planning framework outlined in this chapter is meant to broaden the ways beginning teachers typically plan, which is by thinking about what subject matter they want to teach, and what activities they will engage students in. It's absolutely crucial to also think about the rationale for those choices, and the formative and summative assessments that should be aligned with instructional decisions. Most importantly, teachers must always pay attention to context and tie their planning carefully to the students they are charged with teaching.

CHAPTER 3

Reflecting

Manage Tensions to Reflect on What's Working and What's Not

When I did research for my dissertation in a classroom of 4- and 5-year-old children in Reggio Emilia, Italy, I was unprepared for how life-changing the experience would be. I am convinced this special city, which spreads its approach to working with young children across the globe through countless conferences, publications, school visits, and by helping to build a network of like-minded educators and organizations, is light-years ahead of most educational practice. In an interview with the founder of these municipal schools, Loris Malaguzzi, Lella Gandini (1998) asks him to recount the history of how the Reggio Emilia early childhood schools came to be:

> *A simple, liberating thought came to our aid, namely that things about children and for children are only learned from children. We knew how this was true and at the same time not true. But we needed that assertion and guiding principle; it gave us strength and turned out to be an essential part of our collective wisdom. (p. 51)*

Reflection will bring you liberating thoughts; shared, it brings mutual understanding.

ALTHOUGH IT IS GENERALLY ACKNOWLEDGED THAT REFLECTION is important for improving teaching, there is little shared consensus on the best ways to prepare teachers to be reflective, or to support practicing teachers in their efforts to be reflective. As a result, teachers are often told to keep a journal and to write about their teaching experiences with insufficient guidance on how to do so in ways that will really benefit them and their students. This chapter will show how the strategy of regularly writing and sharing stories about memorable episodes, what are sometimes referred to as *well-remembered events* (Carter, 1993), can provide a structure and focus for reflecting on practice that is theoretically sound and helpful in finding practical solutions to ongoing dilemmas and tensions in teaching. Because these follow a research trajectory of description, analysis, and interpretation, I like to call these reflective pieces *research stories*.

RESEARCH STORIES

What exactly constitutes a research story from classroom life? Let's step outside the world of teaching for a moment to consider an example from a memoir. In an essay by Alice Waters, famous for her Berkeley restaurant Chez Panisse, she recalled an encounter while traveling in Turkey when she and a friend ran out of gas.

> *A shy, big-eyed boy appeared, and he mimed that there was no gas to pump. And we counter-mimed that we supposed we would have to wait. . . . Then, fingers pointing to mouth, where would we get something to eat? . . .*
>
> *Solemnly the boy leads us indoors and into the back room where there are benches against the wall covered with beautiful old rugs, a brazier in the corner made out*

Alice Waters is also known for the Edible Schoolyard Project (see https://edible schoolyard.org) she began decades ago in Berkeley, California.

> *of an old gas can, birdcages hanging from the low ceiling, and a baby brother. Clearly the parents are away and the big brother has been left behind to babysit and turn away customers, and to offer us the imperative hospitality of rural Turkey.*
>
> *The boy builds us a fire out of pinecones, puts on a kettle, and makes us tea. Then he produces a small piece of cheese and painstakingly cuts it into even smaller pieces, which he offers us gravely. . . .*
>
> *He has given us everything he has, and he has done this with absolutely no expectation of anything in return. A small miracle of trust, and a lesson in hospitality that changed my life forever. (cited in McNamee, 2007, p. 36)*

In this short example, we can see the power of such a narrative. First, there is a rich and detailed description of the event. It is perhaps all the more remarkable because the protagonists did not speak the same language and had to communicate with gestures. Second, there is some analysis helping the reader to see the meaning of what occurred, namely that this young boy had learned the cultural importance of offering hospitality to strangers and sharing what little he had to offer. Finally, we see the author's interpretation of the event—a deeply moving gesture of selflessness that taught her an unforgettable life lesson on the true meaning of hospitality.

In the context of classroom teaching, a well-remembered event that is described, analyzed, and interpreted for both personal meaning and sometimes for teaching more broadly, is a very useful tool for reflection. It is "an incident or episode a teacher observes or experiences in a school situation and considers, for his or her own reasons, especially salient or memorable" (Gonzalez & Carter, 1996, p. 40). When

I assigned these short essays to my student teachers, we emailed them to each other and then discussed them in our weekly seminars. I asked student teachers to identify a *single* classroom event that struck them as odd, significant, or particularly memorable and worthy of inquiry for some reason. Some examples of the topics that came up in our discussions of these research stories include

- a student teacher's authority,
- puzzling children,
- disciplining misbehavior,
- adjusting to a new grade level,
- teaching new concepts,
- boy-girl relations,
- parents and family issues, and
- trust and honesty.

Research Story

Describe the event by telling what you observed.

Analyze the event by reflecting on the context in which it occurred, and by reflecting on your growing knowledge of teaching, both from experiences in your classroom, and from the things that you have read about. When appropriate, make explicit reference to any of your readings.

Interpret and reflect upon the significance of the event. Discuss what you have learned about teaching as a result of this event and how you might use what you have learned in your teaching.

Learning to write in this way entails making a concerted effort to begin first with what anthropologists call a "thick description." Perhaps because of the way teachers talk informally with each other and use abbreviated labels for personality types and common classroom mishaps, they fall out of the habit of including descriptive details when writing about events in their classrooms. But it's important to avoid the common pitfall of jumping to conclusions, rushing to judgment without sufficient evidence, and making unfounded assumptions, particularly when writing about behavior and events related to issues of classroom management. The whole point of reflection is to slow the frenetic pace of classroom life down, and to notice what went unnoticed before, like watching a video in slow motion. Think back on how vividly Alice Waters described the room where the Turkish boy invited her to eat; the details of the fire made of pinecones, the hanging birdcages and beautiful rugs, the baby brother, and the meager piece of cheese carefully cut into pieces all make us feel we are in the room.

A research story should begin by helping the reader be in the moment using sensory details and richly descriptive, but not too value-laden, language. If possible, include the talk and conversation as a transcript, and write down what was said while it is still fresh in your mind. You can always come back and elaborate on it later. Although you want to avoid making assumptions, the situated context in which the event occurred, and the fact that you are writing from your own personal perspective, mean that you can't be completely objective and write in a clinical, detached way. Strive to achieve a balance of capturing your memory of what happened, what you were noticing and thinking about at the time, and include those details that seem most important to you.

Another Turkish interior. What details do you notice here? Photo by Ellen Rabiner

The next step is to put together the descriptive details and the narrative account of the episode and then try to make sense of what was going on. Maybe there was a mismatch between what you were trying to convey and what the child was telling you. What might have been the reason for this? Maybe you are writing about a conflict between two students. What preceded the event that might help you understand why their conflict escalated? Do you notice a pattern that reminds you of something you have seen before? How did your expectation of what should happen match (or not) what occurred? What was puzzling or surprising for you, and why do you think that is important? These are some of the kinds of questions you can ask yourself once you have begun to write the detailed description of the episode and want to start to analyze it.

Before writing the last part of the research story, where you will interpret its significance for you personally, and perhaps for teaching more broadly, take a step back and read what you have so far. Think about how a camera lens can zoom out from focusing on one small detail, and try to do the same thing intellectually with your account of this event. How does this detail fit into the larger picture of your experiences in teaching so far? As you have been writing the analysis, and trying to make sense of what was going on, what are you learning about your students, yourself, your classroom, and the contexts that surround you? How is this learning significant and meaningful in terms of learning to become a better teacher? How has it affected your beliefs, and how might it change what you will do in similar situations in the future?

A Sample Research Story

Teachers who do research on their practice and publish their writing about what they learn about and discover through the process of doing practitioner research often use narratives of their experiences with students that are very similar to research stories. One of my favorite teacher researchers, Cynthia Ballenger, writes about what she calls "puzzling moments." She writes, "in order to teach all children more effectively, teachers must develop their curiosity and puzzlement toward children's words and ideas, especially those words and ideas that strike us initially as less powerful and less thoughtful" (2009, p. 8). In an example from her teaching in a Massachusetts preschool where the students were Haitian, she tells a story pertaining to her struggles with classroom management that will serve as an excellent example of a research story and its three components of description, analysis, and interpretation.

> Recently I was angrily reprimanding the children about their failure to wait for me while crossing the parking lot:
>
> *Cindy:* Did I tell you to go?
>
> *Children:* No.
>
> *Cindy:* Can you cross this parking lot by yourselves?
>
> *Children:* No.
>
> *Cindy:* That's right. There are cars here. They're dangerous. I don't want you to go alone. Why do I want you to wait for me, do you know?
>
> "Yes," says Claudette, "because you like us."

> Although I was following the usual Haitian form—rhetorical questions with "no" answers—I had been expecting a final response based on the North American system of cause and effect, something like, "Because the cars are dangerous." Claudette, however, although she understands perfectly well the dangers of cars to small children, does not expect to use that information in this kind of an interaction. What, then *is* she telling me? One thing that she is saying, which is perhaps what the solemn children also meant, is that, from her point of view, there is intimacy in this kind of talk. This is certainly the feeling I get from these experiences. I feel especially connected to the children in those instances in which I seem to have gotten it right. (1992, p. 206)

First, Ballenger describes the moment in which this little conversation took place, and then she analyzes her own thinking in that moment. Finally, she interprets Claudette's comment, hypothetically extending it to the larger context of the other children in her care, as one signaling an intimate connection rooted in care between teacher and student.

Imagine, for a moment, that you were Ballenger's student teacher and witnessed this interaction. It would probably go by in a flash, like many other similar moments when teachers are reminding students of rules or expectations for behavior. Without the opportunity to reflect on the meaning of this moment, Ballenger would probably not have had as informed a way of thinking about the recurring problems she was having with her students' misbehavior. And if you were her student teacher, you probably would not have found it important to talk together about the significance of

Ballenger likes to tackle what she calls "puzzling moments" because she believes the child always makes sense. Photo: *Front cover* (1925-01-10), General Research Division, The New York Public Library. https://digitalcollections.nypl.org/items/1aaa2fd0-1f90-0134-9154-00505686a51c

Claudette's comment. Often when working side by side with veteran teachers, it's hard to see what they see, and therefore it's also hard to talk together about it. It can be equally hard for the student or veteran teacher to accurately describe and analyze layers of complexity in everyday situations that are either troubling or puzzling.

Becoming attuned to potential explorations of research stories, and the sort of careful noticing that such a stance requires, takes some practice. It's a bit like walking in a redwood forest and remembering once in a while to stop and look up all the way to the top of a particularly beautiful and ancient tree and think about what it means to be in the presence of trees that have stood for centuries. If you live in California, in places where the redwoods are plentiful, you might lose that sense of awe that travelers have when they see them for the first time. Veteran teachers can fall into habits and behaviors that obscure what it is that student teachers notice as life in classrooms races by. That is why research stories are also useful narratives to share with others. They can be shared with parents and colleagues as a way to break down the isolation of teaching, and to collaboratively work on solutions to recurring problems and unresolved dilemmas. We'll return to the idea of sharing them with others in the next chapters.

Reflecting on Dilemmas

Once you get in the habit of writing research stories, you may begin to notice some patterns in your reflections. In research that I have conducted with classroom teachers, we found that teachers have to manage ongoing dilemmas in their practice that are different from day-to-day problems, although there may be a relationship between them. A problem, such as two students who, despite requests to desist, continue to have side conversations and disrupt the work of other students around them, might be temporarily resolved by reseating them separately. A dilemma, on the other hand, can be conceptualized as an ongoing tension the teacher feels between potential or performed actions, which only partially manage the dilemma without necessarily resolving it. Each action that a teacher takes or might take along the continuum of the tension presents benefits and drawbacks that have consequences for the goals and aims the teacher has in mind. Returning to the example of students having disruptive side conversations, an underlying dilemma the teacher might experience is a tension between wanting to use teacher authority to take corrective action, and seeing value in letting the students work out a viable solution. If the teacher chooses to use her authority, she runs the risk of little or no buy-in from the students, who may continue their pattern of behavior. On the other hand, if she offers them an opportunity to dream up a solution, which may have the benefit of greater buy-in, there is the risk that they will suggest something that the teacher feels is ineffective. Learning how to manage this kind of common dilemma involves risk-taking, trial and error, and reflection on the results and consequences of particular decisions and actions of both teacher and students.

PROBLEMS have a resolution.

Ongoing tensions are **DILEMMAS**.

Magdalene Lampert has written about managing dilemmas and the tensions she experienced in the context of her experiences as an elementary math teacher returning to the classroom after becoming a professor:

> *In order to do her job, the dilemma-managing teacher calls upon this conflicted "self" as a tool of her trade, building a working identity that is constructively ambiguous. While she works at solving society's problems and scholars' problems, she also works at coping with her own internal conflicts. She debates with herself about what to do, and instead of screening out responsibilities that contradict one another, she acknowledges them, embraces the conflict, and finds a way to manage. (1985, p. 190)*

This way of thinking about managing dilemmas suggests that as classroom events unfold, the teacher's actions are embodied, sometimes improvised and intuitive, and the consequences of those actions cannot be fully reflected on or predicted in advance. For this reason, developing a habit of reflection through writing research stories can lead to moving beyond coping to more finely attuned strategies for addressing dilemmas.

It's important to learn to recognize ongoing, underlying dilemmas in your teaching practice, particularly with respect to issues that seem related to classroom management, so that your practice of regular reflection begins to take shape with purpose and focus. For example, one dilemma might be the tension felt between maintaining a classroom that gives students a sense of safety and security, freedom from teasing or bullying, while also developing a classroom culture that encourages intellectual risk-taking and a willingness to try and fail. David Cohen has pointed out,

> *Instruction of this sort requires that teachers find ways to engage students more fully in learning, but it also requires that they find ways to reduce or otherwise manage the possible personal risks of such greater engagement. It is no mean trick to intensify engagement at the same time as easing its risks. Some teachers and students have worked out strategies to cope with this curious requirement. They have not been much explored, or even described, but there is no evidence that they are easy. (1988, p. 60)*

Can you think of a time when you have experienced this dilemma in your teaching? Perhaps it was when inviting particular students to show their newly explored mathematical thinking at the board or on the overhead, or during a discussion of a literary text that touched on issues of fear and personal harm that could be potentially sensitive topics to discuss as a class. By learning to look for patterns in your reflections, you will become more adept at both recognizing and managing ongoing dilemmas.

Reflecting on Content and Subject Matter

In addition to the strategies of writing research stories and looking for patterns that lead to insights on managing ongoing dilemmas, teachers do a lot of reflecting on the content of what they are teaching. Not only do they develop burning curiosity about topics under study in the classroom; they begin to have specialized knowledge about how to represent and explain certain ideas to students in ways that will make

Burning questions! Where does water go as it evaporates? Why did dinosaurs become extinct? How did we send men to the moon and back? (See *One Giant Leap* by Burleigh and Wimmer [2009].)

sense to them and be meaningful. They must also become experts on students' errors and misconceptions, learning to recognize them and knowing how best to address them. Sometimes it is through their own personal, hands-on learning experiences that they have an epiphany about how to design similar experiences for their students.

Some may wonder why reflecting on content and how students make sense of it is related to classroom management. As we saw in chapter 2, effective planning entails knowing why you are designing learning experiences and how they fit with what came before and what will come. Reflecting on issues of content is important for teachers to do on a regular basis even if they are using established textbooks and curriculum guides to plan their lessons. It's probably true that the experts writing these materials have already thought through the complex issues of learning theories, children's development, effective teaching methods, and so on. As long as you understand the concepts or skills being taught, you may well wonder why you can't just follow the instructional guidelines in the published curriculum. The following cautionary tale will serve as a striking answer.

What habits of mind do you think matter most in teaching?

Make a list to keep by your desk.

Three researchers investigating children's understanding of equality asked them what number would make $8 + 4 = \_\_ + 5$ a true sentence. Most children interviewed in grades one through six answered 12, indicating a misconception of the meaning of the equal sign.

Try asking a child to solve the equation $8 + 4 = \_\_ + 5$ and discuss the strategy used to find the solution. You may be surprised by the answer!

Perhaps due to experiences with endless computation problems on worksheets, these children believe the symbol = means carry out the computation and write down the answer (Carpenter et al., 2003). Surprisingly, fewer than 10% of the elementary students gave a correct answer of 7. Such a basic misconception leads to big trouble when those children begin to learn about algebra and are taught to do the same thing to numbers on either side of an = symbol without really understanding the logic of doing so. This illustrates why teachers have to know the content of what they are teaching with considerable depth and complexity, all the while being attuned to children's developing conceptual knowledge. Even very young children will have questions that require teachers to tap into their personal resources of authentic disciplinary knowledge, pedagogical experience and understanding, and how those two areas intersect in the particular case of specific children.

One of the things that can make teaching so challenging is that certain practices are so common and entrenched it can become difficult to question them or to try to do things differently. In the example of misconceptions about the equal sign, most teachers in the elementary grades are so accustomed to writing math equations with an operation on the left side of the equal sign that they don't notice or maybe even realize the unintended consequences in students' potential misunderstanding of the meaning of that mathematical symbol. So, it's best to start by taking a questioning, almost skeptical stance when using published curriculum. Remember that all of your planning and instructional choices involve your personal knowledge of the context in which you are teaching, and constructing the rationales accordingly. It is a fallacy that curriculum guides will provide all you need in terms of generic content that can be taught in a universally applicable context.

Imagine, for example, asking students to conduct moon observations, and to record their observations and be prepared to share them each day in school. For one thing, as their teacher, you must also engage in looking at and wondering about the moon's appearance. A curriculum guide may contain information about waxing and waning, the moon's orbital pattern, and so on, but you must first and foremost be prepared to engage in conversations about what everyone is noticing. Classroom management, in such a situation, has as much to do with how you are thinking about the content of moon science as how you plan to use ideas proposed by students to develop their theoretical understanding. Trust that students will have ideas about their observations that they will be eager to share, and know that teaching in a way that engages them in exchanging those ideas is exciting; you will have their attention from the start. This palpable engagement will serve you well in terms of keeping behavior problems under control so that you can focus on what students are sharing and understanding.

Let's return for a moment to another example of what this looks like in a real classroom. Cynthia Ballenger, who provided us with an example of a research story earlier, writes about the shifts that were necessary in her practice in order to support the kinds of thoughtful conversations where students began to take ever greater responsibility for the exchange of ideas in discussions. She began to allow for the sorts of things she might normally correct or ignore, such as side conversations, jokes, stories from experiences children had, and metaphors or analogies. In a particularly vivid example, she recounts how this type of participation led to the whole class experimenting with cups of water to observe evaporation. One student, Francois, posed the very real question of how did the water manage to go up, since he observed there was no hole in the cup that would have meant it leaked down and out of the cup. First, Ballenger took his question seriously and accepted that "this was not something we truly understood" (2009, p. 24). Next, the students brainstormed things that can go up. They shared information from a book that stated that heat rises, but this led to other questions such as why mountains are colder than lower ground. They also wondered why, if the water evaporated in the closed environment of the classroom, there wasn't condensation on the windows or ceiling. They observed that water mist sprayed into the air vanished, and this led to numerous other experiments with a terrarium, frozen water melting, and observing their breath outside on a cold day. They also shared their knowledge with kindergarteners and made large diagrams of the water cycle.

Ballenger describes some important outcomes for her own learning from all of these experiences. For one thing, she learned a lot about condensation, and writes, "I think that at that time I was only beginning to recognize from the children's questions how much I didn't know about it" (p. 25). Secondly, she writes that she learned "about the value of emotional and affective connections to subject matter from these children" (p. 25). She also notes that "through their back-and-forth argumentation, they succeeded in developing a much more explicit sense of what growth means in biology" (p. 27). What I think is most relevant for our discussion so far on the importance of reflection, is what Ballenger writes at the conclusion of the chapter:

> *The kids—and it is regularly those kids who are not doing well who have the most to teach us in this regard—looked wrong to me, puzzling and different and not academic, and yet in the end, they helped me to wonder with them about ideas that were long familiar and had lost their mystery, to see the value of the new and*

> *novel connections they were making, to become curious about assumptions I had forgotten I had. (p. 28)*

Similar important revelations are possible for all teachers, and if we have somehow lost our way from seeing teaching in this light, it is certainly not too late to return.

Reflection on one's own practice is important, but so is having a means to process practices beginning teachers are keenly observing in their field placements. Informal experiences can potentially have an even greater impact on student teachers than their formal teacher education (Feiman-Nemser, 1983). One of my student teachers, a pre-K teacher who had taken a leave from her full-time job for student teaching in a first-grade classroom per the state's requirements for certification, wrote of her cooperating teacher's routine for announcing assessment results to the class. Those who moved up to the next reading level or were able to solve a math assessment received applause and congratulations, and then, perhaps with the well-meaning desire to lessen the disappointment of the others, the teacher would read aloud Robert Kraus's *Leo the Late Bloomer* (1971). The research story described how one child "remained silent in a midst of a noisy classroom. His body was relaxed emanating a false air of coolness but his eyes had lost their entire spark. Sadness had stroked this young heart that was usually energetic." The same child had cried the previous week over a math assessment he could not solve. She concluded, "You realize that the general obsession with school readiness has become a cancer that is destroying our children's spirits and our educational system. Children are labeled by a score. Children's ability to become lifelong learners is starting to be crushed by ineffective tools of assessments."

A century ago, the renowned philosopher John Dewey wrote in *How We Think* about a metaphorical way of capturing how we have been describing reflection on memorable teaching moments, ongoing dilemmas, and questions pertaining to subject matter:

> *Thinking begins in what may fairly enough be called a* forked-road *situation, a situation which is ambiguous, which presents a dilemma, which proposes alternatives. As long as our activity glides smoothly along from one thing to another, or as long as we permit our imagination to entertain fancies at pleasure, there is no call for reflection. Difficulty or obstruction in the way of reaching a belief brings us, however, to a pause. In the suspense of uncertainty, we metaphorically climb a tree; we try to find some standpoint from which we may survey additional facts and, getting a more commanding view of the situation, may decide how the facts stand related to one another. (Dewey, 1909/1978, p. 189)*

This is a helpful metaphor for the thinking involved in teaching. Unlike the common understanding of dilemmas, which suggest either having to choose between two equally unsatisfactory alternatives, or simply working toward resolving any persistent problem or fix, Dewey captured the embodied nature of the decision-making process, the desire to see the landscape more completely to make more fully informed choices. Dewey was essentially describing reflective thinking, and to teach well, one must find ways to reflect.

In her teaching and research, scholar Carol Rodgers has developed over many years a structured way of facilitating reflection with teachers that she called a *reflective cycle*. Her initial goals in this work were twofold: to develop the capacity to develop the requisite skills of observation with a critical lens in order to consider not just teaching, but subject matter, context, and how these interacted in the classroom; and to take informed actions based on the growing awareness and professional knowledge of practice (Rodgers, 2002). In slowing down the pace of classroom life, Rodgers found that teachers appreciated the rich complexity that emerged in their inquiry process, becoming more interested and curious about their work. An important component of this type of group learning was a framework for describing and understanding students that grew out of Carini and Himley's work at the Prospect School in Vermont known as Descriptive Review of the Child (Carini & Himley, 2000). In the next chapter we'll take a closer look at the power of those ideas that, if taken seriously at the start of your teaching career, can lead you down a path of deep fulfillment as you seek like-minded colleagues and coaches to assist you in the journey to meaningful growth.

Chapter 4

Knowing Students

Know Your Students Individually and Collectively

Psychologist Haim Ginott was an Israeli teacher who moved to New York and wrote two popular books on parenting before publishing *Teacher and Child* in 1972. His writing is illuminating and driven by a desire to improve communication with young people.

> *What the teacher says about the child touches on deep feelings and hidden fantasies. A concerned teacher is aware of the impact of his words. He consciously avoids comments that may casually kill dreams. (p. 278)*

Most of us can remember favorite teachers, and some we'd rather not recall. Being mindful of the words we use with children is something I have always tried to impress upon my students.

At the heart of teaching, in layers that resonate through all we have discussed so far about planning and reflection, lies the work of developing human relationships that are built on trust, respect, and yes, even love. The best advice I think I ever got, from my mother who has been an educator her whole life, was to work on loving the students who were most responsible for making me feel frustrated and unhappy. Love may seem a loaded word in the context of teaching. Joseph Featherstone describes the democratic vision of education as "true romance" (1995, p. 168). Like Featherstone, when I speak of love, I mean a deeply rooted mutual connection of respect, interest, curiosity; as he puts it, "the romance of respect for the people and what their children's minds are capable of" (p. 168). Particularly when you feel that your troubles in teaching are due to inadequate skills of classroom management, you must dig deep to ask yourself how well you know your students and their families. In this chapter, we will see how the work of Patricia Carini (Carini & Himley, 2000), who developed a process known as the Descriptive Review of the Child at the Prospect School in Vermont, can provide teachers with a framework for studying and understanding children in all their marvelous complexity.

Many people who choose to become teachers describe their reasons for doing so in terms of their interest in and affection for children. After all, children are generally thought of as loving, funny, joyful, spontaneous, engaging, curious, and even adorable. In fact, children may just as easily be aggressive, angry, withdrawn, bored, and whiney. As a teacher, you must accept all children in the full spectrum of their humanity. In all likelihood, you have already developed close relationships with children who are relatives or friends, or you may even have children of your own. Now that you are thinking like a teacher, you will begin to notice more and to see the world more often from a child's perspective, and these observations will serve you well in your own interactions with children. You may find that you have new questions about seemingly mundane moments, like a child's temper tantrum or meltdown in public, or the way two children negotiate the rules of a game they are playing in the park. The more you look, and the more you wonder, the more you will begin to understand how children experience and interact with the world around them.

Children find joy in simple things, especially from the natural world. Photo by Hannah Shin

A teacher's ability to cultivate an ever-deepening recognition of children has never been more important in education. We live in an era of high-stakes testing when children are literally reduced to numbers. To me, there is no greater horror than the callous label of a number or grade to describe a student, and yet this occurs in schools on a regular basis. If not with numbers, students are labeled with one-word empty descriptors like "struggling" or "average." To fight this growing tide, teachers must arm themselves with richly detailed descriptions, anecdotes, examples of extraordinary thinking and participation, and insights into students' minds and lives.

The inappropriate and undue use of standardized tests is unfortunate not only for the dire consequences in terms of accountability decisions and impoverished diagnoses of children's learning needs, but also because all a multiple-choice test question tells us with any certainty is that the student knew to pick one answer out of many. There is no way to know if the student made a lucky guess, or worse, glanced at a neighbor's answer, on the basis of the test score alone. In contrast, a single page of student writing provides a rich source of data for knowing how the student expresses ideas, writes with correct grammar and conventions, and puts together words, phrases, and sentences to communicate. In any given day, there are literally hundreds of opportunities to know more about your students and to use that knowledge to teach them more effectively.

Descriptive Review

Patricia Carini, one of the founders of the Prospect School in Vermont, has written that it takes time and patience to construct portraits of students

> *in which the person is understood to be not the sum of unchanging traits, but in process, in the making. Understood as active and open-ended, each of us is at any moment of our lives, and in all taken together, a complex blend of failings and virtues, of strengths and vulnerabilities. It seems to me that this is what makes us interesting and what makes education (and not merely training) a possibility. (Carini & Himley, 2000, p. 64)*

Learning to use the framework developed under her leadership, for what is known as Descriptive Review, can help you to know your students more fully, and to see them as evolving rather than as static measurements taken in a moment in time. A central tenet of the descriptive review process is to begin with children's strengths and their capacities for meaning making. Another is to engage in the analysis of children's learning and work with other educators and parents to broaden personal perspectives that may unintentionally narrow opportunities for growth.

There are five categories for descriptions and observations of students in the framework. They are:

1. physical presence and gesture,
2. disposition and temperament,
3. connections with other people,
4. strong interests and preferences, and
5. modes of thinking and learning.

These are not necessarily meant to be fixed or discreet categories, but rather useful points of departure for organizing information. There is inevitably an overlap between these categories. How a child moves and with what kind of energy, for example, is connected to his mood and how he's feeling. However, there are ways to generalize patterns of movement and gesture, such as active and fast paced, slow or laborious. As these patterns are noted through observation, they may inform an adult's analysis of a child's typical disposition as reserved or outgoing, upbeat or somber. Carini invites us to picture children in our mind, to call on our memories and observations, in order to concentrate on attending to descriptions that might fit in each of the five categories. This doesn't necessarily happen in a linear, fill-in-the-box kind of way. Rather, as we both notice and recollect the child in outdoor settings, playing and being active, over time we may come to recognize certain preferences for being alone or part of a team, just as recalling the child's physical presence while engaged in a quiet indoor activity, such as drawing from observation, can lead us to know that his concentration and interest can be sustained in certain situations for long periods of time.

What typically happens, as adults use the categories to organize their knowledge of children, is they begin to notice gaps and questions that require further observation and documentation. Knowledge in one category can fuel the need to know more about another category, particularly when making crucial connections between the child's interests and his modes of learning and thinking. Let's say, for example, that I learn from a questionnaire distributed to the class that Jeffrey, a fifth grader, is not especially confident about his abilities in computational math, but he does like working on geometry problems when he gets to use materials like pattern blocks and a compass. In conversing with him about these preferences, I may discover that his mother is an architect, and has given him insights into how the worlds he is discovering in school mathematics are related to how she does her job and enjoys her career. I may come to understand, through observing Jeffrey engaged in academic tasks that tap into his interest in these things, that imaginatively constructing structures and representing them in two and three dimensions is an important mode of learning for his expanding sense of how mathematical knowledge has real-world applications. Now I can begin to strategize ways to build on these interests and strengths to help him gain confidence and greater skill in manipulating numbers, by making them relate to what he knows and enjoys about architectural spaces and structures. It is not very useful, in this example, to label Jeffrey "a visual learner" or a student who struggles with computation, but rather to notice and build on his natural inclinations and strengths to help him see and do more than has previously been possible.

Teaching in this way requires an inner strength, both to persist through initial difficulties, and to resist the growing tide of simplistic labels and problematic use of data. You must first and foremost have faith in your curiosity, your desire to know children and to recognize their fascinating ways of coming to know and understand their world. This curiosity is grounded in profound respect; there is no inappropriate snooping into private spheres, or preconceived prejudices to contaminate the ongoing inquiry. As the noted philosopher Maxine Greene has written:

> *For me, provocative teaching cannot take place unless the teacher's interests are engaged, unless a self in the making is fully present to others—present not only in body but*

What might this image tell us about this child's gestures or strong interests and preferences? Photo by Antonia Balfour

> *also in mind, not only emotionally but also cognitively, not only imaginatively but also analytically. For me, the teacher must communicate a kind of passion—a consciousness of risk and possibility—no matter how much blankness, disinterest, or difference of opinion is expressed by others. (2001, p. 85)*

Do not be alarmed or dissuaded in this pursuit by feelings that you are somehow less objective in your assessment of children if you adopt this stance of respectful curiosity. Unfortunately, even the most renowned universities with legions of educational experts still rely on SAT and GRE scores to sort their applicants. It is risky and difficult to acknowledge that human thought is subjective, but it is also a fallacy to believe that numbers will always be equated with objectivity.

It is also true that working in your own private sphere, and trying to go against the pressures to conform, will feel like swimming upstream and may ultimately lead to total burnout. So, it is absolutely essential to find like-minded others, friends and colleagues who will sustain and support you in your efforts to teach with passion and conviction. We will see in the next chapter how research stories and descriptive review can be used as tools for collaboration and group reflection. For the moment, let's turn to another consideration in the careful study and observation of children: the question of values.

Values and Moral Considerations

Behaviorism has long dominated approaches to classroom management, with a focus on intervention and desist techniques as opposed to proactive strategies for preventing behavioral problems in the classroom. Critics of these behaviorist approaches have pointed out that excessive use of rewards and punishments can undermine children's moral development and sense of intrinsic motivation to learn (Kohn, 1996). More importantly, you must create an alignment between your goals for students, from developing their intellectual curiosity to improving their civic engagement, and the methods you adopt for handling behavior issues as they arise, so that your students don't struggle with conflicting messages about the values that inform the life inside your classroom.

What are some values that are so important they must not only be made explicit, but be upheld by all members of the classroom community? Let me propose a few, and then invite you to think about the values that are most important for you.

- Participation: cultivating a sense of belonging, that everyone's point of view matters, and that decisions impacting the community can be made collaboratively in the spirit of democracy
- Cooperation: learning to work in groups, to solve problems together, and to seek the expertise of others when encountering difficulties
- Diversity: to value difference and subjectivity, to see multiple points of view, to access cultural knowledge from people of all backgrounds
- Caring: learning to treat others with care and concern, to put another's needs first, to provide friendship and support when needed, to be fair, trustworthy, and just in words and actions

Caring for living things in your classroom and taking children on nature field trips can teach them to respect nature and to appreciate the roles they play in protecting the environment.

What other values might be added to this list? Do you value play, and fun? How about equity? What will these values mean in terms of the goals you want to make explicit for yourself, your students, their families, and your colleagues? How can you help everyone to see that these should be and are commonly held values that will inform the way you live and learn together? These are some of the most basic foundations of your whole approach to classroom management.

Clarifying your beliefs with respect to values is particularly important because sooner or later you are going to encounter a situation that will test your resolve to act in the spirit of these values. Children will not always be caring, cooperative, and charming. You inevitably will have to handle a difficulty with aggressive behavior, a student who must constantly test the limits of what is acceptable, or who seeks outlets for personal anger and frustration that cannot be expressed except in physical force. Depending on the contexts surrounding these situations, you may even have to be physically forceful yourself in clarifying where you draw the line, or preventing injury to yourself or others. When you are navigating these difficult waters, do not lose your focus on seeking the student's strengths in the spirit of Carini's framework, and making those explicit to the student in ways that are both sincere and grounded in real, meaningful examples. Then, as you work to restore trust that is the basis of all your relationships with students, bring others in to reinforce the reminders of personal strengths, so that the student can once again return to a feeling of normalcy and participation in the classroom community. These others may be fellow students, other adults in the school, or family members. Particularly when the behavior that is problematic is severe and repetitive, and you convene a conference to discuss the problems together with the student and other adults, do not focus on the negative aspects without balancing the discussion with positive contributions the student has made and can continue to make to the classroom community. In doing so, you will find a personal measure of the type of tone called for in occasions that require sternness balanced with meaningful praise and public acknowledgment of the student's accomplishments.

These moral considerations regarding children with challenging behavior issues require careful attention to families, and to the partnership you form with parents, without crossing the line into overly personal matters. Avoid putting parents on the defensive when teaching children to get along with others; rather, engage in conversations with parents about strategies you can both use to improve the student's prosocial behaviors, conflict resolution skills, and an orientation to the good of the community. Be especially alert to any assumptions you may be making about the home life of children. Be mindful of all influences on children's behavior in school, including video games, playground interactions that may not be attentively monitored, even nutritional considerations. Most important of all, know that you are a moral leader, and set an example for students in your words and actions in the classroom. Gary Fenstermacher has said:

> *What makes teaching a moral endeavor is that it is, quite centrally, human action undertaken in regard to other human beings. Thus, matters of what is fair, right, just, and virtuous are always present. . . . The teacher's conduct at all times and in all ways, is a moral matter. (1990, p. 133)*

There are many ways in which teachers can be hypocritical. They may create rules that speak of respect for others and treating people with kindness, and then in the public space of the classroom persistently humiliate a student who tends to misbehave. They may lecture students who get into personal squabbles on the dangers of gossip, and then turn around and gossip about students and teachers in the faculty lounge. If you avoid these traps and consistently remind yourself that you are a model for others, you will have fewer problems in your relationships and classroom management.

STRONG BEGINNINGS

The start of the school year is a crucial time, for in the first days you will set the tone for all that is to come. The anxiety and stress felt by teachers before the first day of school do not diminish with experience. Students and parents are also full of excited anticipation and hope that the new school year will bring joy, learning, new friendships, and memorable experiences. There are many practical aspects of classroom management that are related to how you set up the physical space of your classroom, and what you do and talk about with students in the first days of school. Remember, too, that you must devote extra time in the first weeks of school to getting to know your students' families and helping them get to know you.

When I was a new teacher, one of my biggest fears about the start of the school year was my inability to remember names. Before school began, I photocopied from the school file pictures of the students who would be in my class, and then made flash cards with their photo on the front and name on the back. They were delighted when we met for the first time and I was able to recognize their faces. I knew a teacher who made a point of calling every student in the class to tell the parents how much she was looking forward to meeting them in person, and then she introduced herself over the phone to the student. You may find that parents and their children, burning with curiosity, drop by on the days when you are setting up your room before school starts. As much as it may feel like an interruption, use those opportunities to spend a few minutes getting to know children and their families. Talk with your colleagues who are familiar with the community and parents, and look over your class list together. They may have had your students or siblings before and have insights into the families you will be working with.

In setting up your room, don't worry if it looks a bit spare. Tell students that soon you will fill the walls with their writing and work, and seek their input into ways to make the room more inviting and attractive. On the first day of school, have them make colorful name tags to attach to desks and cubbies, or to hang over tables. Arrange the furniture so that there are easy traffic patterns, and practice having students move through the space until transitions flow smoothly. Ask for suggestions to make improvements so that students feel involved. Even the dreariest classroom will improve with a few living things. If you don't have a green thumb, try a terrarium; if you are worried about allergies to pets, consider a fish tank or a turtle. Color will also brighten the space, so if you can't paint a wall or a bookshelf, get some wooden crates or a used armchair and paint with abandon. Make sure that basic supplies such as paper, scissors, and pencils are easily accessible and that materials for making things are available and inviting. Set up a recycling center so that students can contribute to stocking the shelves with scraps of beautiful paper, corks, ribbons, small boxes and bottles, and other materials that can be used for art projects. Be sure to make a cozy space for those times when a student needs a bit of privacy and peace and quiet. The more you can involve students in collectively designing and arranging the classroom space, the more likely they are to feel ownership of it and to respect and take care of it.

A classroom should have

- easy traffic patterns;
- accessible and inviting materials for making things;
- ample spaces for student work to be displayed;
- flexibility;

(*continued*)

- print/text, maps, and pictures/posters to look at;
- living things;
- a cozy corner;
- plenty of books;
- as much natural light as possible;
- emergency box with extra clothes, snack bars, first aid kit; and
- identifiable places where things belong and can be accessed by anyone (especially tissues and bandages).

On the first day of school, make sure you smile a lot and make students feel welcome. I don't know who invented that stupid adage to not smile until December, and I can't believe it has lasted this long in teacher lore. Students can get the message that you mean business even if you smile from the start. Your primary goal is to establish in them the conviction that you are a teacher they can trust, and smiling and being friendly are essential ingredients in a trusting relationship. The other thing I recommend, regardless of the age of the children you are teaching, is to play a fun name game. Not only will it help you to remember their names; they will also get to know each other better. The one I have played with success for both children and adults starts with everyone standing in a circle. I demonstrate the premise: first I say my name and let everyone repeat it to be sure they know how to pronounce it. Then I say something that I like that starts with the same letter as my name, such as, "Alexandra likes animated conversations." It helps if this is accompanied by a gesture that makes it easier to remember. Everyone repeats the phrase. When the next person goes, after everyone repeats the phrase, you return to the first person's phrase and gesture and add on the second. As you make your way around the circle, you may try variations such as going backward, or faster, or just doing a segment of the circle. The second part of the game involves a sort of telephone game. The person who begins says their phrase with the gesture, and "calls" someone by saying their phrase. That person answers with their phrase and calls someone else, and so on. A more difficult variation includes a "free" call to a third person; when the second person answers after their phrase they add the "free" call person, and then their own "free" call. The pattern continues as the third person begins with their own phrase, then the previous person's "free" call, and then their own "free" call. Make sure the game is played with abundant laughter and help—the whole point is to build community. It's also fun to see if someone will volunteer at the end to go around the whole circle and say every person's phrase. When they succeed there is always spontaneous applause.

Another important aspect of the first day of school is a discussion of rules. You may be expected to go over general school rules with the class, and even to review certain safety procedures and precautions. When you have time to talk about classroom rules with your students, I recommend inviting them to make suggestions from the start by asking what rules have worked well for them in the past. Try to phrase these rules in positive terms rather than a list of "don't" regulations. Ask them to ponder the kind of classroom environment they want to create with you and to think about features of classroom life that facilitate learning. I worked with a teacher who had fantastic classroom management skills, and successfully maintained peaceful order when students were at work and she was circulating to give individual help and feedback. One technique she used was that she hung some chimes in her room. Anytime the noise level got a little too high, she would gently play the chimes as a reminder to take it down a notch. Any student could also go play the chimes during work times if it got too noisy for his comfort. She also put old tennis balls on the legs of students' chairs to reduce noise in the classroom, and she sometimes played classical music quietly in the background during times of focused independent work. Students were introduced to similar classroom routines a bit at a time, so that they weren't bombarded with rules and regulations on the first day.

In addition to a class discussion about rules, I think it is important to begin the school year with a discussion of goals. You might begin by sharing with students some of your own personal goals for the year, and these may be closely tied to the values that you want to make explicit to them, such as participation and cooperation. Then invite them to write about their own goals, and what they hope to learn and accomplish in the year ahead of them. These should be working documents that you return to frequently, both to see how you are progressing on those goals, and to make revisions or add new goals.

Students will also be curious to explore the classroom on the first day of school, so make time for a tour and some time to wander about. Be sensitive to students who are new to the school and might benefit from a school tour led by a classmate. If possible, take the students outdoors for an activity or game so that they know you intend to make learning happen both in and outside of the classroom. Start something on the first day that will continue into the next day, so they have something to look forward to. I liked to read them a short science fiction story about a man who discovers an alien, stopping halfway through at a cliffhanger moment, and asking them to write what they thought would happen when we finished the story the next day. It's also pleasant to end the day by sharing compliments or appreciations for things people have done. Make a point of telling the whole class how much you have appreciated their help and enthusiasm in making the first day such a success, and that you are looking forward to getting to know them better.

As your room begins to take shape, keep in mind that the classroom environment is educative, and ask yourself what your room says about the kind of learning that is taking place there. How do others describe their impressions of the space to you? What do the students like and notice about it, and in what ways do they demonstrate ownership of it? Have you created opportunities for students to care for the space, to keep it clean and organized, to decorate it, to showcase student thinking and work? What you must also think about is how the space is helping to shape important classroom routines that are also bonding people and developing relationships. For example, Yvonne Divans-Hutchinson, a national board-certified teacher whose important contributions as a teacher leader are detailed in Lieberman and Miller (2005), has a classroom scribe in her ninth-grade language arts classroom who reports on the previous day's events at the start of each class. This not only helps to create continuity from one day to the next; it provides an opportunity for students to practice note taking, public speaking, and expressing themselves with humor, praise, or any emotion called for in the situation. (For a videotaped clip and more information, see her website, http://www.goingpublicwithteaching.org/yhutchinson.) Another example is the use of an author's chair, a place for a student sharing a piece of writing to sit in front of an audience of peers. Even taking attendance in a way that puts students in charge, and maybe introduces some mathematical thinking regarding numbers and arrays, or percentages and graphing, can be a way to create opportunities for learning as well as community bonding.

The Importance of Choice and Natural Inclinations

Finally, there are two more crucial ingredients in helping you to develop positive relationships with your students and their families, and in getting to know them better: *choice* and *natural inclinations*. These two ingredients are connected in that the more choices you provide for students, the more you will learn about their natural inclinations. Remember that the category *interests and preferences*, as we have seen from Carini's framework, is information that will provide clues about the category *modes of learning and thinking*. Giving choices to children is a bit like sprinkling magical fairy dust in the classroom to spread happiness and a pleasurable hum of productivity. Many teachers who regularly schedule an open period where students get to choose from a variety of activities or centers describe it as the most enjoyable part of the day. Children move purposefully to work on their favorite project, and it is possible to structure activities so that they can work alone, maybe even catching up on something that needs finishing, with a partner or in small groups. Choices generate natural motivation and enthusiasm, and these things will reduce behavior problems.

What are some things that children naturally like to do? An expert teacher in Italy who is a friend of mine once noted as we watched 4-year-olds run around the school courtyard, that when given the option, children will always prefer to run. As we become lazy adults, we forget that children love to run, skip, hop, swing, climb, and move around a lot. If your students are getting wiggly, let them stand up and stretch and take a five-minute break, or better yet, let them run around outside. Children are also naturally inclined to want to make things. They like to draw and doodle, paint, sculpt, cut, glue, and construct things using a wide variety of materials. Give them plenty of opportunities to make things and you will find they are more often involved in the task at hand. Let them talk as often as you can. They love to tell and share stories, jokes, riddles, experiences they have had in the recent and even distant past, and they enjoy reading aloud poems and scripts, especially if they get to act them out in front of an audience. Have them dress up, perform songs and dances and plays, play their instruments (no matter how noisy or rudimentary), and give them lots of opportunities to make believe.

If these natural inclinations strike you as too removed from the academic nature of what is expected in school, then focus on a subject area and brainstorm some more natural inclinations. Here are two lists, one for science, one for math, to get you started.

Natural Inclinations in Science

- Examining and interacting with living things
- Using senses to taste, smell, listen, observe, touch
- Looking with special tools like a microscope, magnifying glass, pinhole camera, telescope
- Studying nature photography and taking photographs of the natural world
- Exploring outdoor environments (woods, ponds, streams, beaches, and tide pools)

In one of my favorite schools in New York City, children are allowed to skip down the hallways, which makes for a very joyful vibe.

Natural Inclinations in Mathematics

- Counting, computing, and performing operations with meaningful numbers
- Searching for patterns
- Solving puzzles, strategizing in games
- Identifying combinations and permutations
- Testing probability against real outcomes

As these natural inclinations take root in your curriculum and planning and become an integral part of the classroom climate and culture that you are building, look for opportunities to have students teach each other. Maybe someone has become an expert on weaving friendship bracelets and is willing to lead the class in a hands-on lesson and demonstration, or someone who is bilingual wants to teach the class to say a few things in a foreign language. You can also invite parents and other relatives of your students in to talk about their interests, careers, and travel adventures.

Providing choices that have an impact on parents can also make for improved relations. Maybe that homework packet can be turned in on Friday or Monday, or requests for a home reading log can be sent in on a printed form or by email. These may seem trivial, but you are better off providing the choice and then determining that it doesn't make a difference, than forcing parents and children to comply with what may seem to them an inflexible system. Try to fight any fears or feelings of intimidation that you have about parents, and invite opportunities to know more about their hopes and dreams for their children, their interests in getting involved at school (and there are so many ways besides volunteering to come in during the school day), and personal life experiences and areas of expertise that can be helpful to you in planning curriculum, and to students in learning from them directly. Educators, like anthropologists, have to become experts on people, on their customs, beliefs, behaviors, and so much more if they are to succeed in advancing their knowledge and curiosity about the world.

Chapter 5

Collaborating

Work With Colleagues to Improve School Culture

Maxine Greene was many things to me: philosopher, professor, friend, and source of countless inspiration to a community of artists, activists, and educators who gathered around her in conferences, seminars, and even in the salons she held in her New York City apartment next to the Guggenheim Museum. Her influence is immeasurable, and I cherish my memories of her. In an article from 1993 she wrote:

> *There cannot be a single standard of humanness or attainment or propriety when it comes to taking a perspective on the world. There can only be an ongoing, collaborative decoding of many texts. There can only be a conversation drawing in voices kept inaudible over the generations, a dialogue involving more and more living persons. (p. 212)*

You cannot work alone. Go out and find your collaborators, and make ripples happen.

THERE IS PERHAPS NO MORE ENDEMIC AND PERSISTENT problem in education than the isolated nature of the work of teaching. To be sure, as a teacher you are not as isolated as an office employee in a cubicle, for your days are spent in the company of your students. On the other hand, opportunities for sustained, meaningful, and intellectual interactions with adults are precious few. All too often, the teachers' lounge is poisoned by those who wish to gossip and gripe, and after-school meetings are hijacked by bureaucratic agendas. There are so many competing demands on teachers' time beyond the regular school day: curriculum reformers require professional development sessions; safety regulators require emergency plans; state policy makers want proof of continued learning and teachers' engagement in reform efforts; district and school administrators need help with committee work; and parents want assistance in school governance and decision making. These ongoing demands are taking place against the contemporary backdrop of increased scrutiny on test scores, data analysis, and accountability pressures. It's no wonder the novice teacher feels overwhelmed and unsure about seeking guidance from colleagues—it's practically impossible to find the time to do so even if one were willing to try.

Studies have shown that schools with a strong professional community, where teachers share and learn from and with each other, are much more likely to produce teachers who choose to stay in the profession (Johnson & The Project, 2004). Humans are inherently social, teachers even more so. They do not like to feel alienated and alone. But just because staff are friendly toward one another, that does not mean they are professionally interacting in ways that create learning opportunities for themselves and their students. Moving from a school culture where teachers are merely friendly to one where they engage in critical conversations conducive to meaningful learning and growth may require time and money as a precondition, but it also entails participants who recognize and embrace the value of such an intellectual culture. It also requires a climate of trust so that people are willing to take risks and collaborate with their colleagues (Meier, 2002; Bryk & Schneider, 2002). In an overview of the literature on professional learning communities in schools, Joel Westheimer identified six goals:

> *Educators interested in developing professional learning communities hope to: (1) improve teacher practice so students will learn; (2) make ideas matter to both teachers and students by creating a culture of intellectual inquiry; (3) develop teacher learning about leadership and school management; (4) promote teacher learning among novice teachers; (5) reduce alienation as a precondition for teacher learning; and (6) pursue social justice and democracy. (2009, p. 759)*

As you ponder these ambitious goals, begin to reflect on what you have been noticing in schools, and what might be the areas that are most neglected. See if you can investigate some reasons why that might be.

In this chapter we'll look specifically at how you might use the tools of descriptive review and research stories to work with colleagues on these goals and to build a professional learning community rooted in trust. Learning to collaborate on building a culture that is both intellectual and grounded in common values will help you to feel more confident and successful in your teaching practice, and in other aspects of your career as well.

Start With Leadership

All schools depend on the leadership of the principal to guide key decisions, manage and solve problems, and set the tone for the school culture that everyone must work together to cultivate. Teachers must also take on leadership roles, and not just inside their classrooms. Effective leaders know how to facilitate teamwork, bringing out people's talents, expertise, and passion. They know how to create a work climate in which people are able to flourish. You can tell a lot about a school's climate just by looking around in the classrooms and communal spaces. You will find evidence of the values that are important to that school community, of the work that has been accomplished of which everyone is proud.

You can also help take on a leadership role in your school, even if you are new and less experienced than most of your colleagues. You have fresh ideas, have been learning about and studying recent research and teaching methods, and you bring experiences from another school culture where you were trained that people will be eager to hear about. Teachers depend on the collective wisdom that comes from talking and sharing experiences and perspectives with each other. An expert on teacher learning, Sharon Feiman-Nemser, has written:

> *By engaging in professional discourse with like-minded colleagues grounded in the content and task of teaching and learning, teachers can deepen knowledge of subject matter and curriculum, refine their instructional repertoire, hone their inquiry skills, and become critical colleagues. (2001, p. 1042)*

Of course, teachers like to have someone to talk to about the problems and burdens of their career, and finding an

At first glance schools can look the same, like zebras. Here are some questions to talk about with others: What can you do to make your school stand out? If someone asked about your school's points of pride, what would you share? What are the shared goals that you are working toward with your colleagues and school leaders?

outlet for reducing stress is also important. But if you are to contribute to creating a school culture grounded in continual learning and improvement, it's essential to participate in meaningful intellectual discussions as well. Teachers are more likely to experience greater career satisfaction in schools where there is critical discourse and collaboration among colleagues, as well as trust.

Unfortunately, in recent times school reformers have laid a lot of blame on teachers and have often adopted a tough stance on forcing adoption of what they see as best practice. In her book, *The Death and Life of the Great American School System*, educational scholar and historian Diane Ravitch

(2010) summarizes the reform efforts of two large urban school districts, San Diego and New York, resulting in alienated and frustrated teachers and administrators. This book attracted a lot of media attention because she once supported the policies of choice and accountability, and the politics of No Child Left Behind, and then changed her mind based on evidence that she said was showing these approaches were destroying public schools. Ravitch describes the "corporate model of tightly centralized, hierarchical, top-down control . . . and strict supervision of every classroom to make sure the orders flowing from headquarters were precisely implemented" (p. 73) that was first adopted by San Diego, with Alan Bersin as superintendent and Anthony Alvarado as chancellor in 1998. Then in 2002, the legislature in New York gave control of the public schools in New York City to Mayor Michael Bloomberg, who appointed Joel Klein chancellor. She rightly points out that these business-minded leaders diminish, even dismiss, the importance of listening to the people whose cooperation is a necessary precondition for true success. "They ignored the fundamental importance of trust among those who make schooling effective: students, teachers, principals, and administrators" (p. 66). Raising test scores has become the single most important measure, the one for which leaders and teachers are held accountable, with threats of school closures and layoffs when desired results are not achieved. Ravitch contends that what got us into such a mess is a lack of vision for the purposes of education in our democracy. "The fundamentals of good education are to be found in the classroom, the home, the community, and the culture, but reformers in our time continue to look for shortcuts and quick answers. Untethered to any genuine philosophy of education, our current reforms will disappoint us, as others have in the past" (p. 225).

Another factor that can undermine efforts to work collaboratively is a pervasive American individualism with deep roots in our culture, exacerbated by what some describe as the "egg-crate" environment in schools. Virginia Richardson, a leading expert on professional development, says individualism affects almost everything teachers do:

> *As teachers, the individualistic culture affects the way we think about change, how we seek help for the improvement of practice, who we talk with about what we do in our classrooms. (2003, p. 402)*

Furthermore, she points out that current policies that push for standardization fight against individualistic norms, rather than encourage viable alternatives that would lead to meaningful communal goals and ways to achieve them. Most observations of teaching are centered on providing individualized feedback that often seeks to evaluate the extent to which the teacher is conforming to standardized ideas of so-called best practice. Teachers who wish to resist the notion of standardization may feel such feedback is useless, resenting the evaluation process itself. Instead, we might begin a more public process of sharing lessons that are videotaped, discussing them in small groups, in order to make connections with other experiences and to support learning about the power of collaboration among colleagues.

Clearly, our leaders in education must work together with all educators and the broader community to help create a collaborative culture in schools, one that is in harmony with individuals rather than working in opposition to them, and all constituents must be included and invited to participate. Barriers to effective communication must be identified and overcome. In their book on adaptive expertise needed for effectively leading powerful professional learning in schools, Deidre Le Fevre and colleagues write:

> *Relationships of respect imply reciprocity and include the presence of trust. Genuinely respectful relationships mean that educators value the perspectives of those they work with, creating a sense of mutual safety to challenge each other as well as the knowledge of how much to challenge. (2020, p. 44)*

Creative and energizing ideas are needed to recharge and reframe partnerships among stakeholders in ways that maximize existing resources and make compelling arguments for new funds through grants and philanthropy.

Teachers play a vital role in making these changes happen. Start with small steps. Maybe you will raise enough money to hire a translator so parents who don't speak fluent English can communicate with you on curriculum night in the fall. Maybe you will meet a museum educator at an exhibition opening and make a persuasive case for gaining free admission to the museum for your class, and then co-design experiences to make the most of the field trip. Maybe you will start a brown bag tradition in your school to share students' projects in progress, inviting students, teachers, and parents to listen, learn, and provide feedback. If you are coming up short on achievable ideas, get together with others to brainstorm. The point is, working with people on the goal of a collaborative school culture, and making even the smallest of accomplishments visible to the community will help you develop leadership skills and experience, and will surely lead to greater trust and a clearer vision of the values that inform the desired culture.

Promising Practices

Deborah Meier has written extensively about progressive schools that worked to develop an intellectual, rather than merely academic, culture rooted in trust. She is a firm believer in allowing an intellectual process of willingness and ability to sort through various opinions, find new ideas, listen to others, and to be open to change to develop through having good conversations. In *The Power of Their Ideas* (1995), the students at Central Park East in New York City take center stage, and the book memorably begins with an engaging moment.

> *"Ooh, Daniel," a child's voice calls out, "I've got an idea." Voices pile on top of each other as one after another the children enthusiastically create imaginary worlds, share theories, and act out possibilities. (p. 4)*

The danger of getting bogged down in too many tips for classroom management is that you might respond to such a moment with a reminder not to call out. It's not that there isn't value in creating norms for participation, but as teachers we want to cultivate the sharing of ideas and build on students' enthusiasm for topics and ideas being discussed. Instead of a reprimand, imagine responding by asking everyone to talk in small groups and be prepared to share the ideas discussed with the whole group in a few minutes. Such a strategy involves trusting that the students' talk will be productive, and that the ideas shared will be generative. The fundamental point of departure for rebuilding trust in our schools is to trust in the human desire for learning.

Meier goes into even greater detail, showing what schools built on this premise are like in her book *In Schools We Trust* (2002). The first part of the book conceptually lays out the argument for why trust and cognition are intimately connected, and illustrates some of the challenges in building trust in communities. The second part takes on testing and the dehumanizing effects of the accountability movement and shows how these are undermining trust and feeding public cynicism with respect to public education. In the third part she outlines the implications for scaling up this fragile and difficult work, particularly when it depends on something as complex as human judgment and participation.

In a graduate course I taught where a group of students were reading the book, they asked the class, as part of their presentation on the big ideas encountered in Meier's writing, to divide into three small groups. Each was given a scenario to role-play, based on schools in various levels of transition to building trust. In the first, a school with very little trust, a teacher was attempting a lesson with students who were determined to misbehave in every way imaginable. In the second, a school that was beginning to build trust especially among adults, a conference was in progress with a parent, her child, and a teacher who had concerns about the progress of that student. In the third scenario, a school with a strong culture of trust was engaged in a curricular planning meeting between teachers and specialists. Although this was a simulation, the experiences we had in those groups were very real to us and strongly correlated to experiences we have on a regular basis in schools, as parents and teachers. We were able to feel, and then debrief on, how tensions in situations with little or no trust manifested themselves in our behavior and speech, and how feelings of trust facilitated conversation and open discussion, even when the topic was thorny and difficult. The ways in which the first scenario so clearly showed how techniques of managing students' behavior were largely useless without an underlying trusting relationship between the teacher and her students was particularly memorable. You might consider asking colleagues and your students to try out role-playing in similar scenarios as a way to begin your own conversations on the importance of trust.

How to Do Role-Playing

1. Break into small groups and provide a case or scenario description for each group.
2. Let members of each group decide who will play each role.
3. Give groups time to act out the scenario; cue when it is time to stop and reflect on what they noticed.
4. Share out impressions with the whole group and summarize the experience.

There are several noteworthy ideas about building and developing professional learning communities in schools that are gaining ground in the United States after being developed abroad. For example, in the world-renowned infant-toddler and preschools of Reggio Emilia in Italy,

Role-playing provides an opportunity to see things from different perspectives. The island of Capri in southern Italy looks very different from the water than it does from its peak.

there are two teachers in every classroom who work together to carefully document what students do, say, and create when they work in groups. They analyze it and use the documentation to educate children, parents, and other teachers, and to plan for further curricular experiences. Some of this documentation is published in simple book formats that are available at individual schools, and often it is posted on school walls and in newsletters. The Reggio Emilia approach, as it is referred to, has led to the creation of the North American Reggio Emilia Alliance (https://www.reggioalliance.org), which sponsors conferences and school visits. Researchers Mara Krechevsky and Janet Stork report on many positive results from American teachers learning to use documentation in ways inspired by Reggio educators.

At the Wonder of Learning exhibit (https://www.newyorkcitywol.org) about the early childhood practices of schools in Reggio Emilia, held in New York in 2015, visitors recorded their wishes for children on tags tied to a tree branch.

> *This process also guides the co-teachers in making new hypotheses about the kinds of questions and provocations that will keep the group's motivation high and sustain the children's emotional, imaginative and intellectual engagement. They also make predictions about what might happen next. (2000, p. 59)*

This way of creating and using documentation is very different from current trends in what is called *data-driven instruction*, which is about boosting student performance on standardized tests.

In Japan, a practice known as lesson study, which has been used in this country predominantly in the area of mathematics, involves teachers working together to plan a lesson they will then observe and discuss in a follow-up colloquium. This has created a new norm for observing colleagues as they teach and puts the focus on gaining multiple perspectives on which features of a specific lesson were most useful to students and their learning. More than just another professional development fad, lesson study has spread to over 30 states and is leading to significant improvements in how teachers understand subject matter, instruction, student learning and motivation, and how daily classroom practice is connected to long-term goals (Lewis and colleagues, 2004).

A decade of research projects in the United Kingdom, known as the Teaching and Learning Research Programme, found, among other things, that a narrow focus on learning outcomes was damaging to teachers' resilience and professional identity, and that it was important for values to be the subject of professional discussions.

> *It is important for teachers to be provided with opportunities to undertake reflective, collaborative, classroom-focused inquiry in order to develop a well-informed approach to their own learning journey or trajectory. (McNally & Menter, 2009, p. 942)*

In a survey of over 1,200 teachers working in high-needs urban schools in the United States, results indicated that there was a strong association between effective teaching as measured by student achievement gains and opportunities for building and sharing collective expertise among teaching colleagues (Berry and colleagues, 2010). The implication in these and many other studies is that teachers who don't have opportunities to benefit from working collaboratively are more likely to burn out and leave the profession altogether.

Next Steps

So, even though there are good reasons to hope you will teach in a school where professional learning communities are valued and are flourishing, you may also find that there is still a persistent undercurrent of guarded privacy, a reluctance to discuss difficult issues, and a general lack of opportunities for intellectual debate and engagement on ways to improve teaching and student learning in your school. In this next section, I will return to the strategies of descriptive review and research stories to suggest how you might use those together with your colleagues as a way to overcome some of these obstacles to a collaborative culture. I will also talk about how to start doing more co-planning and team teaching, which may be another way to work toward that goal. My suggestions are not meant to downplay the value of going to a trusted colleague with a specific problem related to classroom management, but rather to create a more sustaining collegial support system that is mutually beneficial to all participants and keeps the focus on specific students and their learning, rather than just your performance and management strategies.

What will help your efforts to make time to meet with other teachers to talk, plan, reflect, and share is to create an openness to questions. Julie Diamond, an early childhood teacher researcher, has written that her weekly meetings with two colleagues created a form of professional development that "was a place to *ask* questions—not a place to answer them. We opened questions up and let those questions lead us to other questions. And it was possible to do this as we built up trust in each other" (2008, p. 321). Teacher groups, especially smaller and more intimate ones, should avoid the tendency to jump in with advice and instead take time to explore problems, stories, and observations of students from multiple angles and perspectives. You will see things in a new light, and may discover that your beliefs or assumptions were getting in the way of figuring out the right course of action to take.

Try This

- Meet with a group of teachers and generate questions about things that are puzzling or difficult for you.
- Write each one down on a separate sticky note.
- Post the notes on a board and work together to cluster them into groups.
- Discuss how you might label the groups that were generated.
- Turn this into a working map for the areas you want to work on together.
- Revisit and revise the map as you move forward.

Teacher groups that have endured over time and published accounts of their work together share the protocols for their meetings that they have found helpful. For example, Cynthia Ballenger describes her work at the Cheche Konnen Center in Massachusetts (2009) in which monthly meetings typically consisted of two threads: ongoing work on science investigations conducted by teachers; and sharing classroom transcripts or videos (see also Rosebery & Warren, 1998; Ballenger & Rosebery, 2003). Once the transcript was chosen, based on a concern or question for the group, or simply because it was an exciting discussion, each participant would be assigned a student to focus on before watching the video or reading the transcript. After viewing the episode, the transcript would be read aloud as a script. Discussion would then begin as teachers tried to describe the ideas and perspective of their focal child. Staying close to the words in the data kept the spotlight on students and less on the teacher. Ballenger wrote, "It was also a way to make sure that even students who said little received a fair share of attention" (p. 81). Groups that focus their discussions on transcripts of classroom episodes sometimes develop their identity around that work, such as the Santa Barbara Classroom Discourse Group in California, a collaborative community of teachers, students, and faculty from UC Santa Barbara using ethnography to study education.

Descriptive Review

In teacher groups that adopt the Descriptive Review of the Child, there is a presenter as well as a chair. It can be very helpful to ask someone to be responsible for writing up narrative notes on the meeting. These not only create a record; they signal the importance of participants' contributions. Sessions sometimes begin with a reflection on a keyword, followed by the chair's remarks to frame the session's focus. The presenting teacher follows the five categories for descriptive review and shares other salient details such as the classroom environment and daily schedule, and speaks without interruption from participants. The chair summarizes the presentation in what is sometimes called an "integrative restatement" and asks for any additions from other staff before inviting discussion and facilitating dialogue around the focus questions. The chair also has the important role of summarizing main themes, responses, and recommendations from the group's discussion, and inviting an evaluation of the process from participants. Variations on this protocol have developed as teachers find ways to make the process suit their particular contextual needs. For example, the Whittier Inquiry Group of K–6 teachers in Chicago created a modified protocol based on six steps: data presentation; describing noticings; raising questions; reflections and wonderings; sharing from the presenter; and a discussion of implications for teaching and learning (Ballenger, 2009, pp. 82–83). In my graduate courses, when we tried out a variation on these protocols, students said they found that time flew by because they were talking about something everyone cared deeply about, and the discussions were very engaging.

Research Stories

In addition to using descriptive review, as described in chapter 4, I have also had small group discussions in my student teachers' seminar meetings that centered on sharing weekly research stories. These were written up as short essays of a few pages and emailed to everyone in the group ahead of our meeting. Each teacher took a turn summarizing and commenting on the research story, and then we took time to talk together about its significance and personal relevance for us and for teaching more broadly. Our discussions of these stories enabled us to touch on so many varied topics and issues, and to begin to see the interconnectedness of our questions regarding students' behavior, motivation, performance, and the curriculum, teaching methods, and subject matter. We also were learning to hold back on interpretation until we had done the hard work of detailed description and analysis. The habit we developed of analyzing a micro look into classroom life on a regular basis over time led to important insights and understandings about the macro aspects of teaching. Margaret Himley, who has written about similar approaches in her Syracuse Writing Program's "Political Moments Study Group," found their discussions inevitably led to larger issues of democracy and power.

> *Sustained, structured conversation based in storytelling proved to be an excellent method for establishing a collective context for learning about the many dynamics of power involved in trying to have a democratic classroom. (Carini & Himley, 2000, p. 204)*

I think it's important to make writing a component of teacher group meetings. Without the discipline of creating and sharing a written record, it's too easy to fall back on turning the meeting into a sharing session that lacks intellectual rigor. Creating a written record also means you can look back on an archive over time and see how far you've come, which can be very gratifying. This is also the first important step in publishing your writing.

A former student who had taken the course offered at my college based on Joyce Epstein's work (Epstein & Sheldon, 2023) on family school community partnerships (see https://nnps.jhucsos.com) published an article on her experiences as a student teacher in Queens, New York, in the local chapter newsletter for the New York Association for the Education of Young Children (https://nyaeyc.org). In her conclusion she wrote that she

> *realized that my job was much more than instructing students. I was struck by the feedback I received from parents at these community-run events. They felt grateful to their children's teachers that the gates of communication between school and home were opened, allowing information to pour through and subsequently the child's needs to be addressed in a variety of ways by numerous caring adults. The teacher is suddenly no longer alone in their journey of educating a child.*
>
> *As the catalyst in developing these lines of communication, the teacher plays a key role in the process of building family-school partnerships simply by reaching out. The partnerships that are established represent additional pillars of support in the foundation of a child's education, a foundation that will greatly strengthen my ability to do my job well in the classroom.*

Teachers must try to carve out time to put their ideas in writing and share them with others. As my former student noted, teachers are catalysts for change.

To summarize then, here are some suggestions for getting a teacher group off to a good start:

- Make an invitation open to everyone; you don't want to create negative feelings of exclusivity before you even begin.
- Pick someone to be a facilitator for each session, to both guide the discussion and help stick to the agenda.

- Have a written record of some sort for every session (minutes, notes, transcripts, research stories, and so on).
- Make time and room for lots of questions and don't feel they all need an answer.
- Develop a protocol for your meetings that suits your needs and context, and be open to revising it as your group sees fit.
- Establish appropriate norms for confidentiality and ethical considerations.
- Maximize your face-to-face time by sharing documents ahead of time.
- Always leave time for a brief evaluation of the session so you can collectively work on making improvements for next time.
- As your group grows and develops, consider seeking funding for additional meeting time such as a weekend or summer retreat, or a series of professional development days.

Most importantly, be content to start small. It will take patience, time, and hard work to develop a group that can satisfy the needs of its participants.

Team Teaching

If starting a teacher group seems too ambitious an endeavor, you might consider another popular form of collaboration, namely team teaching. This usually involves some co-planning, collaboratively designing academic tasks and assessments, and then either teaching side by side with both classes of students or sometimes swapping classes with colleagues. It's fun to try out multiple strategies and experiment with different formats. Mostly, you will likely benefit from seeing your students with another teacher and from working with another class, and they will benefit from the refreshing change as well. In the elementary school where I taught sixth graders, my two colleagues and I each designed a two-week unit to do with our classes. We carved out a common time in the month's schedule when we could take turns rotating all three classes through, so for two weeks I had one colleague's class, and the other class for the remaining two weeks. This also gave us the opportunity to teach the same unit twice in the same month. Ordinarily, this doesn't happen, and it's a powerful way to focus on making nuanced revisions that improve your teaching and the learning experiences you provide for students. The sixth graders loved it because it gave them a taste of what middle school would be like with different teachers for each subject. With another colleague, we sometimes put our two classes together to explain a group activity we were going to work on, and then created mixed groups with students from both classes to work on a project together. This can also work successfully by pairing older students with younger students, which is sometimes called working with "buddies." Older students enjoy helping younger ones with everything from reading to playing math games.

Another idea to try with colleagues from different grade levels is to create a choice time. Each teacher offers to teach something about which they are especially passionate. Parents can also be invited to teach a small group. Students sign up for the group they are interested in, so teachers end up with a mixed group of students from multiple classes and grade levels. These choices can be designed as a one-time lesson or a multiweek unit. There are many benefits to heterogeneous groupings of students, and it can be refreshing for everyone to take a break from current obsessions with grade level and achievement measurements. It also creates opportunities to create interdisciplinary curriculum and to integrate the arts into learning experiences that students of all ages will enjoy.

Of course, there are also inclusion classrooms where teachers with different expertise are paired up to provide additional support to students with special needs. There are some schools where team teaching and even multiage grouping are built into the design and philosophy of the school, so teachers can benefit from sharing responsibilities, and in some cases, getting to work with students and their families for more than one academic year. There can be some perils in situations where teachers are put in the same classroom and may have friction that is difficult to resolve, or teaching philosophies and styles that do not blend easily. Student teachers do not typically have a choice of cooperating teacher, so sometimes these tensions are felt even before having your own classroom. It's up to everyone to be honest about what isn't working and to use administrators and colleagues to help find solutions.

Collaboration taps into the fundamentally important social dimensions of learning. When you are struggling as a beginning teacher with issues you believe are connected to classroom management, it's often not enough to get advice from a more experienced colleague or from an administrator or coach. You need a deeper intellectual engagement that emerges in conversations where classroom life is scrutinized, analyzed, and interpreted from multiple perspectives. You need to be able to watch your colleagues as they teach, and to talk together about what you noticed and wondered about. You need to be able to pose questions without fear of ridicule or embarrassment, and to try to solve problems in a climate of trust and support. Collaboration is the space in which the previous ideas we have explored about planning, reflecting, and knowing your students and their families all come together. By making inroads in ways both small and large to generating more opportunities for collaboration in your school, you will also find that a school culture begins to take shape and form that is grounded in trust, respect, and faith in the human desire to learn.

CHAPTER 6

Theorizing

A Metaphorical Look at What the Research Says

If you want to work on getting smarter, you have to read. Not just for pleasure, but to challenge yourself, to have ideas to talk about with others, to see yourself as the intellectual you are. David Cohen was a professor of education and policy at the University of Michigan when I was there, and his wife, Magdalene Lampert, was my teacher and on my committee. His wonderful short book titled *Teaching and Its Predicaments* (2011) takes you on an enlightening journey into his thinking about teaching.

> *It takes both generosity of spirit and the capacity to put oneself in learners' intellectual places for teachers to consistently try to see things from learners' perspectives. Yet teaching and learning will not go well unless teachers also have a clear sense of quality work. They must cultivate a sort of dual consciousness: on the one hand intellectual selflessness as they seek to learn what sense students make of material and use that learning to inform teaching, but on the other deep knowledge of the material and a clear view of the nature of good work. (p. 185)*

Don't be afraid to be the teacher who is always checking all sorts of books out of the library. It's an important place to feed your mind and find the ideas that keep you moving in a forward direction.

Chapter 6

Despite the overwhelming amount of advice available to educators and parents on how to foster a positive learning environment for children and avoid disciplinary problems, it remains an elusive goal for many adults. The situation has taken an ominous turn in recent times, particularly following the gruesome incidents of gun violence not just in high schools, but in middle and elementary schools as well. Public opinion is shaped by the sensationalistic coverage of such events in the media. When the teacher-student power struggle was captured in the 1955 film *Blackboard Jungle*, with Glenn Ford and Sidney Poitier, the violent confrontations, rebellious students, and racial tensions were shocking to the public at the time. Seeing the film today, though, gives us pause, for aren't students still trying to gain control of the classroom? Does today's violence suggest that things have really changed so dramatically in recent years? Is it so difficult to point to concrete examples of progress, both in terms of theoretical developments and understandings and in terms of classroom practices that show there is a better way?

My purpose in this final chapter is neither to provide an exhaustive review of research and literature related to classroom management and discipline, nor to adequately map out the field. That has been done elsewhere (see Charles & Senter, 2008; Doyle, 1986; Duke, 1979; Good & Brophy, 2003), and has been eloquently examined and critiqued (Butchart & McEwan, 1998; Kohn, 1996). Of particular interest is a more recent review that focuses on the written contributions of teacher researchers to understanding how practitioners examine classroom management issues in their classrooms. Kim Fries and Marilyn Cochran-Smith found that other research on classroom management "will always capture only part of the story about how teachers manage to teach" and that context is embedded in teachers' accounts (2005, p. 975). Rather, it is my aim to choose representative samples from the vast array of approaches to understanding and examining classroom management and sociocultural climate, and to explore how they might be grouped and compared through the metaphorical conceptions of the classroom and school that emerge in these selected texts. From various genres of writing about the topics of discipline, classroom management, and climate, including textbooks, practical teaching guides, and research articles and books, a select few will be discussed and analyzed through four categories of metaphors for elementary school. The goal, in this critical look at a selection of literature on the topic, is to show that at the heart of the climate and management issues lies the very conception one holds of the classroom, and it is this conception, here explored with a metaphorical frame, that can shape the life inside a classroom.

It is still commonly believed that good classroom management is synonymous with good teaching. Dan Lortie, in his seminal sociological study of teaching (1975), noted that when teachers were asked to recall important mentors in their own learning experiences, the standouts were those teachers with good interpersonal skills. Even when asked to identify qualities of good teaching among their peers, teachers pointed to the ability to establish positive relationships while maintaining control:

> *The outstanding teacher not only produces learning and the love of learning but evokes respect and affection, high*

> *effort from students, and compliance with classroom rules. The outstanding teacher, past or present, manifests classroom leadership; the qualities cited suggest a degree of personal charisma. (p. 120)*

Questions about what exactly constitutes quality teaching are still being debated today and will most likely continue to be a matter open to interpretation. But evidence continues to point to management issues as those most likely to be used by evaluators to determine the effectiveness of a teacher's leadership in the classroom, and teaching guides and textbooks aimed at preservice teachers provide just such a cautionary tale:

> *First,* classroom management is possibly the most important challenge facing beginning teachers. *A new teacher's reputation among colleagues, school authorities, and students will be strongly influenced by his or her ability to perform the managerial functions of teaching, particularly creating an orderly learning environment and dealing with student behavior. (Arends, 2001, p. 156)*

Beginning teachers are often overwhelmed by the myriad approaches to classroom management, and are sometimes misled by well-intentioned experienced teachers into the belief that only with efficient authority and control can the work of teaching begin. Rather than getting lost in the maze of alternative strategies and approaches, beginning teachers should reflect on their own metaphorical conceptions for classroom life, so as to make informed choices and decisions about organization and the relational features of teaching.

HISTORICAL BACKGROUND

Research and theory development on classroom climate and management issues have been dominated by a psychological perspective that seeks to understand both the technical skills that are effective in managing student behavior, and the group processes that make for a smoothly run classroom. As noted previously, classroom management has often been equated with classroom discipline, with a focus on what teachers should do about students who misbehaved. Some writers find it useful to separate the two; others blend them. Walter Doyle felt the two had to be understood together, even though for certain purposes it is necessary to separate them. He wrote: "Misbehavior and what teachers do to stop it are not an isolated entity in a classroom. Rather they are part of the fabric of the ecological system that defines and sustains order" (Doyle, 1986, p. 418). Alfie Kohn, a vocal critic of systems of rewards and punishments, speaks to the entangled nature of the definition:

> *Contrary to claims often made in its behalf, it does not merely signify a set of procedures that enable educators to more effectively reach any goals they may happen to have. The very idea of classroom management, far from being neutral, enfolds within it certain goals. And these goals may well be seen as highly problematic. (1996, p. 56)*

Revisiting his ideas 25 years later, Kohn noted that when questioning the underlying assumptions of classroom management, a different view comes into focus, one that is based on caring communities and providing choices (Kohn, 2021). Because classroom management and discipline are both controversial and tenuously defined, it is worth considering briefly the impact of some historically significant research in the field by those commonly acknowledged as foundational thinkers.

Jacob Kounin's research in the 1960s differed from much experimental research popular at the time in that he sought to observe in classrooms and interview teachers as well as students in an effort to understand differences between effective and ineffective managers (1970). One question guiding Kounin's five-year study in college, high school, and elementary settings was whether the methods used by teachers to handle misbehavior affected the students' responses, and surprisingly Kounin found that what he termed "desist techniques" were not significant determinants of successfully managed classrooms. He concluded: "Whether a desist is effective or ineffective is *not* dependent upon the qualities of the desist technique as such (except for anger producing discomfort) but rather upon other dimensions of classroom management, related commitments, or prevailing variables" (p. 73). Kounin also pioneered the use of videotape to study and compare elementary classrooms that were more or less successful in involving students in their work, and in a second study identified dimensions of group management that "far outweigh disciplinary techniques in their power to influence the behavior of children in classrooms" (p. vii) and furthermore were related not only to the management of misbehavior, but also to increased work production on the part of students. Although Kounin did not invent these dimensions or categories, he did give them names that continue to be influential in teacher preparation programs today. They are *withitness*, or the proverbial "eyes in the back of the head"; *overlapping*, meaning attending to more than one thing at a time; *smoothness*, and avoiding getting sidetracked; *momentum*, or the pace and flow of a lesson; *group focus*, ensuring students know what to do and why and are accountable; and *anti-satiation*, providing variety and intellectual challenge in classroom tasks. Kounin's major contribution was the notion that good classroom management was more dependent on effective ways of preventing misbehavior and problems than on how such misbehavior was handled by the teacher once it occurred.

Walter Doyle built on the work of Kounin by theorizing elements of all classrooms that affect participants, regardless of who they are or how they are taught. These were *multidimensionality*, referring to the large number of events and tasks in classrooms; *simultaneity*, and the notion that many things are happening at once; *immediacy*, which adds the notion of a fast pace to simultaneity; *unpredictability*, especially given the high number of interruptions and distractions in classrooms; *publicness*; and *history*, which has to do with accumulation of experiences in a classroom. Doyle's important review of classroom activities (1986), which summarized his work as well as that of others, pointed out that all classrooms are organized by activities, distributed into various segments, and by participation structures such as teacher lecture, seatwork, or small group work. Doyle's contribution was to enlarge our conception of the role of organization and management in classrooms, and to see how academic work itself was both "an important dimension of the program or vector of action in classrooms and a significant factor in accounting for how classroom life is organized and how order is achieved" (p. 407).

One final important historical note was the contribution of the 78th yearbook of the National Society for the

Study of Education edited by Daniel Duke (1979), which was entirely dedicated to classroom management. Duke defined classroom management as constituting "the provisions and procedures necessary to establish and maintain an environment in which instruction and learning can occur" (p. xii) and sought to include in the volume's overview not just psychological perspectives, but sociological and organizational theorists' ones as well. The final chapter by John Goodlad commented on the "problems and dilemmas involved in seeking scientific underpinnings for the practice of classroom management" (1979, p. 391) and noted the lack of comprehensive theories that would encompass the many elements managed in classrooms. He felt that future directions for theoretical work should be directed at generating, rather than confirming hypotheses, and that while much emphasis had been placed on the academic goals of schooling, little attention had been paid to three other goals, namely vocational, social-civic, and personal. Goodlad argued for the value of theoretical bias and spoke to his own ecological orientation to examining schools. He concluded with two suggestions for making research and theory development more useful to practice. The first was for "conclusion-oriented researchers" to engage in more holistic, natural, and ethnographic research in classrooms, and the second was for "decision-oriented researchers" seeking improvements and reform to collaborate with like-minded teachers, so that productive work could be accomplished toward possible theories of "good" practice (1979, p. 407).

THE USEFULNESS OF METAPHORS

In a seminal book by noted linguist George Lakoff and philosopher Mark Johnson, the authors begin with the premise that a metaphor is more than a poetic device, but rather "is pervasive in everyday life, not just in language but in thought and action" (1980, p. 3). Their purpose is to painstakingly show through examples that the processes of human thought are metaphorical in nature for the most part, and that metaphorical concepts are systematic and pervasive. If we accept that metaphors, both explicit and hidden, shape the way we see and act in the world, and help us to more carefully attend to both the nature of the world around us and how we come to know and understand it, then we might find it useful to examine the issues of classroom climate and management through a metaphorical lens. The metaphors that abound in educational writing will not necessarily lead us to a single theory of "good practice," but they can illuminate aspects of teaching that have become taken for granted or obscured. We have seen in previous chapters that there is much to learn about teaching that is not readily visible to those at the start of their career. Robert Boostrom pointed out in an article that examined the use of the "safe space" metaphor in education that the use of a particular metaphor did not mean we could improve teaching or our understanding of teaching. He cautioned, "To use a metaphor is not a way of *doing* teaching; it is a way of *talking about* teaching . . . [metaphors] tell us how teachers see themselves, their students, and their work" (1998, p. 397).

Robert Bullough (1994) has argued that the root metaphor that has most strongly taken hold in education is the "school as factory" metaphor, "an especially robust weed" (p. 7) whose persistence he sees as troubling. "From the factory metaphor other metaphors flowed that defined the proper role and relationship of teachers and students in school, most prominent among them discipline and management" (p. 1).

Like other critics of mainstream approaches to running the classroom, Bullough takes issue with management and discipline, both factory-like metaphors, for the social philosophy they imply, with grades as wages, material rewards for good behavior, and tracking as just a few of the consequences:

> *In simplified form, principals are managers charged with making certain the system runs smoothly, that nothing disrupts the flow of the day. Teachers are more or less skilled assembly line workers and are responsible for meeting, not setting, production goals. Quality standards are set outside of the school. Students are products to be molded and shaped in predetermined ways; education is something done to or for them, not by them. Lack of efficiency in a production sense—more units for less money—is the most serious educational problem allowed by the metaphor. Discipline is about achieving control for the sake of efficiency. Competition is highly valued and there must be winners and losers. Losers, who represent defective material, are removed from the assembly line and discarded or subjected to inferior treatments from those who represent better quality material. Especially good material might be treated differently as well, by being specially certified and allowed to continue on the line longer, with the expectation of greater rewards. (p. 3)*

Such a startling comparison begs a critical scrutiny, not only of the teacher education texts criticized by Bullough for their unquestioning stance on these issues, but also of texts produced in research communities. The factory metaphor is not only troubling; for some it is downright offensive. As Gary Fenstermacher and Jonas Soltis point out in their

The factory metaphor for schools has been compared to an "executive approach" to education. Photo: *General View Sewing Room—Large Shoe Factory, Syracuse, N.Y.* (1895). The Miriam and Ira D. Wallach Division of Art, Prints and Photographs: Photography Collection, The New York Public Library. https://digitalcollections.nypl.org/items/510d47e1-5f02-a3d9-e040-e00a18064a99

book *Approaches to Teaching* (1986), the characterizations of what they describe as the "executive approach" offend our sensibilities about education, which we do not want to equate with life in factories or on slave ships. "Yet the executive approach invites comparison to such things. It stresses attention to task, performance of duty, achievement results, and accountability for failure to produce" (p. 16). The factory metaphor is certainly tenacious in education today, and we shall see how some of the analogies summarized by Bullough emerge in another classroom metaphor that has grown out of this root metaphor.

School as a Military Institution

The structure of the hierarchical power relationships as well as the ambitious production goals found in the factory metaphor can be found in military education, with its ranking system, its clearly drawn portraits of the good soldier, marine, or naval officer, and its highly structured training programs. Although the influence of the military's approach to education may at first seem less obvious in today's public schools, the strict discipline, highly structured learning sequences, and competitive spirit endorsed by the military are certainly present in many schools.

The school as military institution has even been taken literally in a California charter school called the Oakland Military Institute (see https://www.oakmil.org/). The idea belongs to Oakland's former mayor, Jerry Brown, who persuaded the California Board of Education to grant the school a charter, and got $3 million from the US Department of Defense and the California National Guard. Over 600 sixth through twelfth graders are currently enrolled, 75% are Latino and African American, and their school day begins with military drills at 7:45 a.m. run by sergeants from the California National Guard, who are each assigned a classroom "platoon" to help teachers by mentoring students. Dressed in strictly regulated uniforms, students, called "cadets," are subjected to rigorous discipline in their platoons, based on an elaborate system of merits and demerits, and cadet promotions. The school has graduation rates of 90%.

Less literal applications of the military metaphor abound in public education, from zero-tolerance policies to required school uniforms. But how does the metaphor emerge in classroom management texts? Most notably, militaristic language and ideas appear in approaches to discipline that stress the overarching authority of the teacher and the goal of getting students to obey and comply with the teacher's rules. Because of criticism that such programs are too authoritarian and obedience driven, many now carefully couch such language in terms of getting students to *choose* to comply and to behave properly. Just as the military seeks to inspire each new cadet to internalize the ideals of the military (see, for example, http://www.usma.edu), these programs use carefully constructed systems of rewards and punishments to persuade students to do the right thing, namely comply with the teacher's requests.

Of these programs, the best known and most widely used is Lee and Marlene Canter's *Assertive Discipline* (1992). They believe that to create an optimal classroom environment, "you must increase your ability to influence your students to behave, in spite of the problems you face at school, and in spite of the problems students bring with them to school" (p. 3). Many a Hollywood film has been constructed out of the notion of the troubled, lost, disrespectful, sorry excuse for a human being who is transformed by the military training experience into a hero, *in spite of* his or her problems. The Canters' beliefs about discipline in schools are grounded in the notion, highlighted in their text in colored boldface, that "children are not innately motivated to behave in school" (p. 7). Furthermore, they feel that parents no longer reinforce good behavior at home as they used to, when they "warned their children about the consequences of misbehavior—and they backed their words with action. Children knew that if they got in trouble at school, they'd be in twice as much trouble at home. . . . They came prepared to behave" (p. 6). In order to behave, the Canters feel, students need four things: to know the teacher's behavioral expectations; to be given limits; to receive positive recognition and support; and to be taught how to choose responsible behavior (1992). These needs are met when the teacher adopts an assertive style, as contrasted with a nonassertive response style, or a hostile response style. If the teacher explains clearly and confidently her expectations, and is prepared to back up her words with actions, then students will trust and respect her "because they clearly know the parameters that have been set for acceptable and unacceptable behavior" (p. 38).

Also key to the Canters' discipline advice is the development of clear and observable rules. In the elementary grades, some general rules they suggest include "no swearing or teasing" and "no yelling or screaming" (p. 53). In the US Army's athletic programs, the cadet-athletes are expected to be positive role models who exemplify good character by exhibiting respect and courtesy, exercising restraint in actions, making only positive comments about other athletes, institutions, and coaches. In the Canters' program, positive recognition is advocated to prevent misbehavior, but when that fails, students must face unpleasant, though not physically or psychologically harmful, consequences. The Canters recommend a "discipline hierarchy" so that the first time a student breaks a rule, a warning is issued, the second time it happens, the student is moved away from the group for 5 or 10 minutes, the third time, for 10 or 15 minutes, and the fourth time, parents are called. The "severe clause" is to send the offending student to the principal (p. 88). In the case of the army's athletic programs, it is the executive director who handles all alleged violations of the code of conduct, and who has the authority to issue a directive to take action on the violation. This action is also hierarchical, and "may include an admonishment or warning, a private or public reprimand, suspension of any person from attendance or participation in one or more events or games, forfeiture of any game or other actions as the Executive Director deems appropriate." These parallels are striking, for in both cases the rules are explained in terms of what is unacceptable, and the consequences are both hierarchical and determined by a single authority.

The question of whether public admonishment is potentially psychologically harmful to students has been a major problem for the Canters, for they became well known for a technique designed to help teachers keep track of students who broke the rules in which the student's name was written on the board for a warning, and then progressively checks were added next to the name for repeated offenses. Landau and Stollenwerk (2000) recount how a seemingly reasonable management idea could have devastating consequences in practice. For example, a school psychologist in the Midwest found a student's name on the board with 31 checks next to it. Teachers also found that the same names would appear on the board, and that the effectiveness of the technique quickly dissipated. A teacher's narrative account of the failure of this and similar techniques is described in detail in the fourth chapter of Daniel Meier's book, *Learning in Small Moments: Life in an Urban Classroom* (1997). The Canters felt they were misinterpreted, in that the purpose of the checkmark system was not public humiliation, and now recommend that the teacher keep track on a clipboard and "calmly say, for example, 'Janet. You talked out. That's a warning'" (1992, p. 90). Landau and Stollenwerk point out that when students are singled out, whether for good or bad behavior, teachers "risk losing whatever general goodwill they are attempting to foster in their classrooms" and students are not helped to feel safe (2000,

p. 155). Others disagree, and feel that clear expectations and public consequences for rule infractions show students that the teacher cares. Regardless of where one stands on this debate, the issue of when and how to single out students in a classroom appears in other metaphorical conceptions of the classroom, but the notion of *public* rewards and punishments is key to the military metaphor. This is what will lead students to make good, rather than poor, choices about their behavior and participation in the classroom.

In contrast to the military metaphor and other examples that fit the teacher-as-effective-authority paradigm that dominates much of the writing about classroom management and creating a climate conducive to learning, there is a growing body of literature that turns instead to the cultural contexts that play a vital role in the establishment of roles and relationships in the classroom. As we move ahead to look at other metaphors where culture plays a central role, it is useful to keep in mind James Peacock's idea that culture has to do with understandings and codes that a group learns and shares, and that these are often tacit or taken-for-granted, yet powerfully influential (1986).

School as Home

Books written for beginning elementary teachers often address the issue of classroom climate with explicit home metaphors. For example, some recommendations for setting up the classroom include using home furniture and accessories in classrooms, such as couches, beanbag chairs, floor pillows, area rugs, table lamps, and plants, and having a speaker on hand for soft background music. One such guide even states, "Perhaps the best model of relationship and the social skills and actions that go with it is to consider the classroom as your living room, your students as neighbors and friends" (Kovalik, 1997, p. 21). In her vision of an ideal "schoolhome" inspired by Maria Montessori's *Casa dei Bambini* (Montessori, 1964), Jane Roland Martin points out:

> *A homelike area does not transform a school or even a classroom into a home. And it was not the furniture that made the* Casa dei Bambini *a child's surrogate home. One dwells in a house. One feels safe, secure, loved, at ease—that is, "at home"—in a home, at least in the kind envisioned by Montessori. (1992, p. 12)*

Helping students feel safe from threats, supported by their peers and their teacher, and in general cared for are common indicators that many see the classroom as homelike in Martin's sense, and not just because the classroom environment isn't sterile and sparse. For a better understanding of how the home metaphor emerges in texts about classroom management issues, the teacher research genre is useful not only because the teacher's proximity to and deep knowledge of students is indispensable, but also because we can find rich narratives where this metaphorical notion of home is often found.

Cynthia Ballenger's book, *Teaching Other People's Children* (1999), is about her three years in a Haitian neighborhood's Catholic preschool in Massachusetts as a teacher in a bilingual classroom. As the only one in the school who was not Haitian, Ballenger describes the cultural lessons she learned and hurdles she had to overcome in order to understand "what counts as knowledge in the classroom and my own attempts to evaluate this in light of daily encounters with these spirited and hard-thinking children" (p. 6).

Noted early childhood educator Maria Montessori (1870–1952), who was trained in medicine, created what she called *Casa dei Bambini*, or Children's House, in Rome and developed an approach to teaching that incorporated many practical activities found in the home, including cooking and gardening. Photo: *A Little Girl and Boy*, Carl H. Pforzheimer Collection of Shelley and His Circle, The New York Public Library.

In the fourth chapter, Ballenger directly addressed the management problems she encountered in her classroom of Haitian children, whom she points out are often difficult to control when their teacher does not share their culture. "The children ran me ragged. In the friendliest, most cheerful and affectionate manner imaginable, my class of 4-year-olds followed their own inclinations rather than my directions in almost everything" (p. 31). Noting that her Haitian colleagues did not have similar problems, Ballenger turned to them for advice:

> *Colette told me I loved the children too much. I asked her if she didn't love the children. She agreed that she and*

> *the other teachers did love the children, but she said I let them know it. I asked her if the children didn't know that she loved them. She agreed that they did. We could not figure out what it was I needed to know. (p. 32)*

Ballenger began to write down the texts of what the Haitian teachers said to children when directions were given beyond a simple, one-word direction such as "stop" in an effort to get at their particular values and intentions. One adult recounts how she reprimanded a child who kicked her teacher, by asking if her mother or her father allowed her to kick at home. When the child answered no, the adult told her, "You are taking good ways you learn at home and not bringing them to school. You're taking the bad things you learn at school and taking them home. You're not going to do this anymore. Do you want your parents to be ashamed of you?" (p. 34). In a similar vein, when Ballenger's colleague Colette was reprimanding a group of misbehaving children, she asked them about their interactions with their mother:

> *Colette:* When your mother talks to you, don't you listen?
>
> *Children:* Yes.
>
> *Colette:* When your mother says, go get something, don't you go get it?
>
> *Children:* Yes.
>
> *Colette:* When your mother says, go to the bathroom, don't you go?
>
> *Children:* Yes.
>
> *Colette:* You know why I'm telling you this. Because I want you to be good children. When an adult talks to you, you're supposed to listen so you will become a

> good person. The adults here like you, they want you to become good children. (p. 34)

Furthermore, Colette revealed that instead of trying to interpret the reasons for a child's misbehavior for him, she would remind him that she's his friend and "we don't do that." Ballenger came to see that a characteristic of American teachers was to focus on the individual student, while Haitians emphasized the group and the responsibilities of belonging to and participating with the group. Although both American and Haitian teachers made references to families, Ballenger noticed the Americans tended to look at specific characteristics of a child's family, while the Haitians noticed what families had in common. "The families do not differ in their desire that the children respect adults, that the children behave properly, and that their behavior not shame them. The children's answers . . . present a vivid enactment of the sort of unity this approach at times engenders" (p. 36).

Ballenger struggled to conquer her own socialization, and to try on the Haitian style of interacting with children who were misbehaving. As she noticed improvements, she also discovered she loved experimenting with the Haitian approach. She began to notice the significant impact it was having on her relationships with the children:

> *I was struck by an experience I had one day when I was reprimanding one boy for pinching another child. I was focusing, in the Haitian manner, on his prior, indisputable knowledge that pinching was simply no good. I also used my best approximation of the facial expression and tone of voice that I see the Haitian teachers use in*

> *these encounters. I can tell when I have it more or less right because of the way the children pay attention. As I finished this particular time, the other children, who had been rapt, all solemnly thanked me. They were perhaps feeling in danger of being pinched and felt that I had at last been effective. This solemn sort of response, however, has occurred a few other times. Their solemnity in particular gives me the sense that these situations are very important to them. (p. 37)*

Ballenger is metaphorically positioning students' behavior at school with their behavior at home.

That the ties to home are important for any teacher to understand is widely acknowledged, but what is more complex is what to do about a significant mismatch between the teacher's cultural background when it stands in marked contrast to that of the students, who may represent dozens of differences in race, ethnicity, religion, class, and so on. Ballenger is able to show that "the area of misbehavior and the way it is responded to seems particularly important because it affects so directly the nature of the relationship between child and teacher" (p. 38). That she does it so clearly may be due in part to the fact that she was teaching in a monocultural context. Nevertheless, her caution about the tension between the two cultures' notions of individual and community responsibility merits careful consideration. She warns, "It appears that Americans do speak as if something like the child's 'enlightened self-interest' were the ultimate moral guidepost. In comparison with the language used by the Haitian teachers, there is very little emphasis on shared values, on a moral community" (p. 40).

Ballenger's examination of these issues helps clarify not only the important role of the home culture in the classroom, but also how the classroom culture is like that found in homes and families where people are close, share hopes and dreams, and experience unique intimacy.

In his important book, *Life in a Crowded Place*, Ralph Peterson asserts, "It is by establishing values of caring and trust in the classroom that social ties and interest in one another's welfare comes into existence" (1992, p. 13). Caring and trust are common themes found in the school as home metaphor. Noted philosopher Nel Noddings believes caring derives from a feminine orientation to ethics, and her work adopts a relational definition of caring. "To feel safe, secure, and cared for—characteristic of dwelling-as-residing—gives children the courage to wander forth both physically and intellectually into new territory" (2001, p. 104). But what does the literature say about how a teacher can go about establishing such values? One important and recurring element is the sharing of personal stories. Peterson calls this phenomenon "talk story," and says that in many ways it simply resembles what friends do when they get together. The purpose of such moments in the classroom, which often happen gathered in a cozy spot first thing in the morning, is not necessarily to develop ideas for writing or to improve communication skills, but rather "to experience the presence of one another, to listen and enter into the ordinary and extraordinary story worlds that are made. . . . There is a coming together when people in a learning community intertwine the events happening in their lives through story" (1992, p. 49).

A teacher researcher who captures this aspect of life in classrooms vividly, and who explicitly uses the home metaphor in her study, is Carollyne Sinclaire, who draws on three years of teaching third, fourth, and fifth graders in northwestern Canada (1994). Driven by a need to understand what it was like to be a student in her classroom, Sinclaire began to wonder about the nature of home, which she felt "provides us with the sense of communion with others that helps the individual self emerge. . . . Home calls to each of us as a search for the familiar, the intimate, the safe, the place where one can take risks, fail and be accepted back in" (p. xix). Sinclaire describes how at times the stories emerge unexpectedly, but listening carefully has lasting consequences. John, a difficult boy who is often "pounding, poking, grabbing, kicking, shrieking, even farting" sits near his teacher at a table after yet another aggressive spat with a girl, and begins to tell of his many moves to new towns, and of the difficulty of being in seven schools since kindergarten. He goes on to reveal much about himself and his family, and Sinclaire discovers this shared moment enables them to "achieve a certain intimacy. In listening, I hear his pain and uprootedness and, as a result, I see him differently. John, too, is changed in the telling and in being heard" (p. 38). Lamenting the fact that her university education never suggested she should listen to students' stories, Sinclaire writes of how her listening helps her to understand how they make meaning of their lives.

Another anecdote about an incident during Sinclaire's ritualistic morning sharing helps to illustrate the sort of understandings that are built in a community where stories are often shared. Judd, angry about an invasion of personal space, curses out loud at Roey. Sinclaire, in a nonthreatening tone, says she couldn't hear what he said and could he repeat it please. When he does, she responds, "You said that?" which prompts Judd to laugh as he admits, "Yeah."

> "Judd calls me that all the time," Roey rejoinders, his head on one side.
>
> "And that's not all," Allan adds, his eyes bugging out. "Judd's got more. He always says . . ."
>
> I start laughing, and so do the other students. We are laughing at the absurdity of the words.
>
> A few minutes later we are all sharing inane, insulting remarks and chuckling together. Finally, there is a lull in the insults and a few quiet moments for reflection. "They really don't mean very much, do they, Ms. Sinclaire? I mean, they're just names, aren't they?" Andrea asks. (p. 65)

After they agree that insults can be funny and silly but can sometimes hurt, there is an extended period of silence as Sinclaire describes an atmosphere where thoughts and memories "resonate within us in the contemplative mood of the room. . . . I hope the atmosphere of that silence lingers long enough for my students to know that conflict can be resolved through discussion; that confrontation can be avoided; and that humor and understanding can result" (p. 65).

Sinclaire feels that the relationships between students and their teacher build the classroom atmosphere through the reciprocal dispositions of emotions and feelings. This atmosphere is not confined to the walls of the classroom and must include perspectives informed by life at home. For Sinclaire, "to teach is to search and discover what is unique and different about each child and to attempt to enhance this uniqueness" (p. 78).

School as Democratic Community

While the home metaphor stresses the value of caring, trust, and building relationships of mutual respect, what is less clear is the role of community, and the implications of democratic ideals of justice, freedom, consensus building, and leadership through selected representation for life inside classrooms. These themes emerge from some classroom climate literature in a metaphor for school as a microcosm of the larger democratic society. As Peterson points out,

> *When community exists, learning is strengthened—everyone is smarter, more ambitious, and productive. Well-formed ideas and intentions amount to little without a community to bring them to life. . . . Although the concept of community in the classroom is not new, what is new is insight into why it is so important. We know now that the way human beings learn has nothing to do with being kept quiet. It has to do with our desire to make sense of our experiences, to join with others, to become a part of a community. (1992, p. 2)*

Such values as civic responsibility, respect for diverse viewpoints, freedom of expression, and others, are those that, proponents argue, are critical to the livelihood of a healthy democracy, and should be part of the fabric of life in schools.

Perhaps no one has made the argument for seeing the school as a democratic community as passionately or as vocally as Alfie Kohn, a full-time writer and lecturer who appears often on television and radio programs and is frequently mentioned in newspapers and magazines. Kohn questions the entire discipline enterprise, and feels strongly that the fundamental compliance goals of most discipline and classroom management programs are deeply misguided. "After all, if a good society was defined as one where citizens obey any and every governmental decree, then scholars might be able to adduce scientific evidence that a good leader is one who resembles Orwell's Big Brother" (1996, p. 55). He advocates a rejection of traditional teaching methods, and believes strongly in the value of a constructivist approach to teaching for alleviating problems that lead to chaos in the classroom. Also key to Kohn's vision is the importance of giving children a say in the governance of their lives in classrooms. His suggestions are gaining popularity, particularly his guidelines for holding regular classroom meetings, which is not a new idea, but which has been given a renewed purposefulness in Kohn's writing. Meetings, he argues, are not only places for sharing personal stories, but also for deciding, for planning, and for reflecting on the day-to-day activities in classrooms. Mostly, Kohn is an advocate for creating a climate of connectedness. "Virtually any meaningful long-term goal we might have for students requires us to attend to the climate of the school and, specifically, the extent to which children feel related, as opposed to isolated" (p. 102).

No teacher researcher has captured the dramatic effectiveness of the classroom meeting for building a democratic classroom community quite as compellingly as Mona Hajjar Halaby, a third-grade teacher in Oakland, California. Frustrated by the constant interruption of conflicts among her students, Halaby decided to adopt a classroom meeting model because her goal was for her students "to experience self-determination and to share the power of daily classroom management. I also wanted to create a class community where the children experienced a sense of belonging, where they felt connected, and where they were encouraged to care about one another" (2000, p. 124). Halaby's democratic orientation is evident in her explanations to children:

> *"You see, Pasong, when you've got lots of power, you become responsible for others. You need to treat them well. In order to be a good leader you've got to include your friends in the process of decision-making. That's what a good president does, that's what a good teacher does."*
>
> *Time to involve the whole group. "Tell me, children, what are the qualities you look for in good leaders?"*
>
> *"They're nice to you."*
>
> *"They're fair when there's a problem."*
>
> *"They listen to you."*
>
> *"They don't boss you around all the time." (p. 13)*

Halaby does not gloss over the difficulties of trying to manage a classroom democratically. When a boy publicly reveals that another boy in the class has touched him inappropriately in the groin, Halaby writes, "I had no control of this meeting. No foresight, no hindsight. No time for a plan, for a course of action. Just barreling down with speed" (p. 23). Summarizing her account of this incident would not do it justice, for it is masterfully crafted and its deep meaning is a result of her detailed narrative. Even as Halaby arrives at the end of the school year, things fall apart and she has to investigate the causes by calling for an "emergency" meeting. Reminding them that their classroom was "like a home" and that it deserved respect, Halaby asks the students what has happened to their self-control. Eventually, during the last meeting of the year, Kate reveals that she thinks they were wild because "we wanted to pretend it didn't matter to leave our class." Another adds, "I wish I could be in third grade forever" (p. 117).

This study provides an important reminder that teaching children democratic processes and values in the classroom is an ongoing challenge, and that their learning is sometimes fragile. More studies are needed that show how democratic processes develop and are achieved in classrooms and schools, particularly with young children. While there is ongoing research on dialogue and discussion, particularly in secondary social studies classrooms, it is rare to find systematic and long-term studies in the primary grades. An important exception is a study by Louise Jennings and two teacher researchers at the Center for Inquiry in South Carolina (Jennings and colleagues, 1999). They sought to address a gap in the research noted in a review of research in multicultural education (Grant & Tate, 1995) that found there were few empirical and systematic studies of democratic processes and their underpinnings in classroom practice. They adopted a notion of democratic teaching practices that values and supports students "in *observing, acting upon*, and *creating* their lived worlds in *response to* and *in concert with others*" (Jennings and colleagues, 1999, p. 2), and then sought to discover what was accomplished in class discussions, beginning on the very first day of first grade, and following the students through to the end of second grade. Combining ethnographic methods with discourse analysis in a methodology known as interactional ethnography (Castanheira and colleagues, 2001), they were able to show how the teacher afforded students multiple opportunities to learn about their responsibilities for shared learning, the importance of interacting with each other, and the role of caring in learning, and how the students "brought to the conversation actions of observing each other, interacting and responding with kindness, and taking responsibility for shared learning" (Jennings and colleagues, 1999, p. 8). Another important finding was that building a democratic community and the academic work of the classroom were not two separate entities but were jointly accomplished. Furthermore, they found that "constructing spaces for dialogue is important but insufficient without considering the types of interactions involved." Students must be given opportunities to develop practices in classrooms that emphasize "observing and action upon the local world in a humanizing capacity" (p. 13).

Another ethnographic study that focuses in particular on developing such sensitivities in students and involves them in the broader community beyond the school walls is called *Forging an Educative Community* (Romano, 2000). Rosalie Romano seeks to make visible, through narrative details of a third-grade classroom's inquiry into homelessness, what exactly constitutes an educative community that fosters both intellectual and social growth. Once again, the theme of connectedness is central to a conception of a democratic community.

> *Using Storyline, a structured, active approach to learning, students and teacher develop relations of trust, compassionate imagination, sense-making that foster a sense of belonging among the teacher and children. Relations predicated and built upon these dimensions are critical attributes to an educative community for they actually strengthen and deepen what is learned. (p. 4)*

Maya Lin's Civil Rights Memorial in Montgomery, Alabama. In my fifth-grade class, we studied Freedom Summer using Storyline (known also as Storypath), creating young adult characters traveling to the South to help voter registration efforts in 1964. The experiences we had helped forge an even stronger community.

Romano describes the teacher's role as a listener and facilitator as crucial, for he must locate jumping-off places for topics that merit further inquiry as they emerge in discussions, and then guide "students into habits of inquiry, dialogue, and into a companionship of learning together." This is a vision that sees teaching a curriculum as "part and parcel of paying attention to students as complex, capable, growing human beings" (p. 57). It also sees that the purpose of education is first and foremost to connect an individual's personal growth with social life in the public sphere.

Some have taken the democratic community metaphor to mean that all decisions in the classroom are reached by majority rule, or that an elective process must be used if students are to perceive a fair and due process for selecting students for various tasks. Given today's diverse student populations, it is often forgotten that what is best for most is not necessarily best for all. Teacher researcher Simon Hole (1998) gives a cautionary account of a colleague who finds herself faced with a dilemma when she wants to democratically elect student reporters for the school newspaper, and finds that the majority vote approach is in direct conflict with her desire to capitalize on one usually disengaged girl's interest in the position. Stating that she couldn't stop herself from going ahead with the vote because "we had worked too hard establishing the purpose and importance of the democratic process" (p. 415), she is nevertheless crushed by her decision. Hole reflects on the dilemmas inherent in teaching, in trying to balance the needs of individual students and the needs of the group, as he poses his colleague's dilemma to other teachers. Sensing that teachers often fall back on a default position of control to ease the tension of such dilemmas, Simon concludes with an anecdote of just such a situation in his own classroom, but he leaves an intriguing unanswered question dangling: "What if tension itself is essential to the process of learning for both our students and ourselves?" (p. 419).

SCHOOL AS THEATER

This issue of tensions in the classroom, particularly between individual and group needs, comes clearly into focus in the school as theater metaphor. Such a notion of life in classrooms is not that new (see Starratt, 1990), and teaching itself is sometimes thought of conceptually in terms of artistic performance (Sarason, 1999). Given the fact that elementary classrooms are places where dialogue, storytelling, and narrative sharing usually occur every day, it is easy to see the logic of the theater metaphor. Vivian Paley's writing about her kindergarten classroom shows her theatrical orientation, for nearly everything is seen through the storytelling lens as she explores issues of race (1979), inclusion (1992), gender issues (1984), and so on. Theatrical metaphors appear in her preface to Halaby's book:

> *The seven- to ten-year-olds we are about to encounter are actors in a classroom story of theatrical dimensions. The stage business seems simple enough: children enter complaints about one another into a communal notebook, then come together every Friday to plead their cases. The plot that develops, however, captures our attention with remarkable intensity. (Halaby, 2000, p. ix)*

In *White Teacher*, now considered a classic teacher narrative by many, Paley describes her volatile relationship with a black boy in her class who is very aggressive and curses a lot, and how the usual behavior management strategies of praise, punishment, or even ignoring bad behavior failed miserably (1979). Finally, almost by chance, she tries a new strategy, and allows Steven to say "fuck" twice a day, and "shit" twice a day, but once he has reached that limit, he's told, he can't say those words again that day. Not only did Steven manage to eliminate the racial epithets and cursing from his vocabulary as a result, Paley noticed, "he was using different language to express some of his feelings" (p. 21).

Those who embrace the school as theater metaphor see the teacher's role as one of opening up language possibilities and enabling children to more fully express themselves, and to explore their identities in their interactions with others in the classroom. Karen Gallas, another primary grade teacher researcher who, together with Cynthia Ballenger, was part of the Brookline Teacher Researcher Seminar, has closely examined the narratives in her classroom and believes that she is a better teacher as a result of her inquiry. "For children, meaning is built into stories; they use narrative to construct mental models of their experience, to make the world they inhabit sensible" (1994, p. xiv). She expands on the idea of narrative as only written or spoken, and she examines how they tell stories in "dramatic play, in their drawings and paintings, in movement and spontaneous song" (p. xv). Gallas also takes a risky stance as a researcher, for she seeks out tensions, puzzles, dilemmas, and difficulties as points of departure. "My stance as a teacher-researcher often begins by situating itself in an attitude of not knowing and loss of control, not in a physical sense, but in the existential sense of losing control of the meaning of habitual practices" (p. 9). She finds that such a stance opens her imagination and enables her to see the innate order and logic of classroom events, once she pushes past her own lack of understanding or confusion, even though she often finds "the children, the teacher, the data, the process, and even the question are all constantly changing and rearranging themselves in different relationships" (p. 9).

A dilemma that Gallas has taken on in her research and teaching is one that resonates for many teachers. It is the problem of what Gallas calls "the bad boys" who like power, and through language, seek to control classroom dynamics. She uses "bad" purposely because it is a public stereotype of these kinds of boys, but her writing pleads their case that "they are an underserved and misunderstood classroom population" (p. 51). As her inquiry progressed, Gallas developed a conceptual framework that grew out of the school as theater metaphor, and it includes "the idea of *performance* as a way to view children's actions, children's assumption of *personae* as a means to try on different social roles, and *topography* as a way to characterize the social terrain of each classroom community" (1998, p. 29). Noting that some children shifted personae and experimented with different characters even within a given day, Gallas found her approach encompassed fictional performance, and one that represented a developing public identity. "It is both an imaginative act and a representation of what is real in the child's life, and it includes an acute awareness of audience. Often this public character provides a direct contrast to the child's private or personal self" (p. 6). The bad boy role is a seductive one, for bad boys enjoy lots of attention, and are both admired and feared, although Gallas found that maintaining the high status required a lot of energy and tended to isolate them from the classroom community. "In my experience these boys are experimenting with the character of the bad boy to see how it fits. They walk around in the character for a while and play with the kind of power it provides" (p. 36). Gallas began to change her interactive style, and rather than forbidding the bad boy behavior, tried instead to respond as a participant, pointing out (often privately) what she noticed, "both to make them aware of the results that I was observing and to begin to have them clarify what they really wanted to have happen socially" (p. 41). As she began to uncover the distinctions between their public selves as actors on the classroom stage, and their private selves, and to look at them more carefully, she found it easier to effectively "intervene in their public behaviors with knowledge about their private selves and the kinds of experiences they valued" (p. 43).

The drama of the bad boys is played out in an extreme case of a teacher working in a residential and day school for boys with severe emotional and behavioral challenges in a study by Joseph Cambone (1994). Anne is an accomplished teacher of special needs children with five male students, ages 5 through 8, who were acknowledged to be the most violent and disturbed boys ever enrolled at the school. "Taken on their own, they are difficult to manage, demanding, and impulsive; put together, they interact explosively, provoking each other in a variety of ways—fighting, striking out at adults, throwing furniture and objects, and running away" (1994, p. 218). The challenges faced by Anne as described by Cambone are almost inconceivable, and his narrations of classroom events are both riveting and heartbreaking. As he writes at one point, "The heart of this school beats fast, pushes hard; it is difficult not to get caught up in the rapid-fire thinking, talk, and movement" (p. 225). The process of getting the boys acclimated to the classroom is painfully slow, even though the events described by Cambone often move with breathtaking speed. A seemingly smooth and calm lesson on apples, for example, dissolves into theatrical pandemonium in a flash:

> *Paul leaps up to run from the room but Cathy grabs him. Samuel starts rocking back and forth, head like a rag doll. Paul is yelling, "Fuck you, leave me alone, fuck you." "Paul, you have to the count of three to be back on your bench or you will leave the classroom. One, two." Paul stops screaming and cursing, smiles at his classmates, cocky. Samuel gets quiet but then laughs and seems like a willing participant in the misbehavior. "Now the whole group is going to sit." When they hear this, the room bursts*

> *into chaos again. Paul grabs his crotch wildly and starts shouting suggestive words. Samuel laughs hysterically. Paul lifts his shirt and displays his stomach provocatively to Samuel, sing-songing, "BELLYBUTTON!!" Anne takes his arm and begins to remove him. (1994, p. 223)*

Anne's belief in the boys' capacities to learn and to improve sustain her as she slowly moves them toward increased skills and capabilities to participate in the classroom life they construct together. Unlike so many people who work with troubled children and focus strictly on behavioral outcomes, Cambone shows how Anne "exhibits a respect for disturbed youngsters' intellect and ways of thinking, while negotiating with them the path of learning without a loss of rigor" (1994, p. 129).

Anything But Simple

We have seen how a metaphorical exploration of conceptions of school and classrooms has enabled a particular view of the last few decades of research on classroom climate and management. This view has shown the complexity of these issues and the multilayered roles and relationships in classrooms that create that complexity. As Duke said over forty years ago, "In short, classroom management, although a very practical, 'real-world' issue, is anything but simple" (1979, p. xi). The purpose of this exploration has not been to suggest that one metaphor is better than another, but rather that uncovering the metaphors leads to theoretical insights into why these issues of life in classrooms are key to creating a positive learning environment. David Tuohy, who has written of the invisible aspects of teaching, finds that "exploring the metaphor and applying it to education can reveal assumptions about teaching and learning, about the organization of the school and the role it plays in society" (1999, p. 62). In particular, he looks at three metaphors, school as garden, orchestra, and factory, to show that although there are areas where all three metaphors overlap, each one comes to stand for a particular aspect of schooling. In a special issue on metaphors in the education journal *Theory Into Practice*, guest editor Hermine Marshall pointed out that a heightened awareness of the role played by metaphors in influencing thinking about teaching and learning "will lead to deliberate reflection concerning the effects of metaphors we routinely use as well as to a search for new and more powerful metaphors to guide educational improvement" (1990, p. 70).

In the case of this investigation of classroom management and climate, we have seen how the military metaphor

Some days school can feel like a carnival ride.

emphasizes control, discipline, and assertive authority, while the home metaphor emphasizes caring and trusting relationships in an environment relatively free of threats. The democratic metaphor values community and connectedness, while the theater metaphor stresses interpersonal dynamics and the relationship between public and private personae. In these times of increased accountability in education, and the push to establish standards for both teachers and students, it sometimes seems we are on the fast track to sameness. Exercising our imaginations and exploring the personal and collective meanings we find in metaphorical concepts of school and the classroom might derail us for a moment so that we can fully consider the consequences of where we are headed. Bowers and Flinders cite a warning to teachers from poet Robert Frost, who, in an essay titled "Education by Poetry," cautioned:

> *[If] you don't know the metaphor in its strength and weaknesses, you don't know how far you may expect to ride it and when it may break down with you. You are not safe in science; you are not safe in history. . . . All metaphor breaks down somewhere. That is the beauty of it. It is touch and go with the metaphor, and until you have lived with it long enough you don't know where it is going. You don't know how much you can get out of it and when it will cease to yield. It is a very living thing. It is life itself. (cited in Bowers & Flinders, 1990, p. 23)*

Looking Ahead

As you continue to make your way through the maze, forging a path ahead by embracing uncertainty, building relationships, and deepening your knowledge both practical and theoretical, I have a final bit of advice. Before I began my own journey in education, I worked for the news organization Reuters. As a result, I developed a daily habit of checking international headlines. Often the news is depressing, and to keep myself from getting too down, I find I have to skip over some of the more gruesome details and aspects of what happens regularly on our planet. In education, following the news is daunting, for so much is happening, and it varies widely from place to place. Just keeping up with your own local context can be challenging. I do have a particular favorite source of informed reporting: a podcast called *Have You Heard?* by my friend Jennifer Berkshire and her academic historian partner, Jack Schneider. They have also published two important books, *A Wolf at the Schoolhouse Door: The Dismantling of Public Education and the Future of School* (2020) and this year *The Education Wars: A Citizen's Guide and Defense Manual* (2024). They should be on your podcast playlist, and you will learn from their many carefully selected guests what is happening on the ground. They have a way of helping you situate the current crises in historical perspective, which for me at least, can be reassuring. Surrounded by ancient stones and Roman ruins in my current home city, I often look out in wonder at the beauty and think to myself, *this too shall pass.*

References

Anderson, L., & Stillman, J. (2011). Student teaching for a specialized view of professional practice: Opportunities to learn in and for urban, high-needs schools. *Journal of Teacher Education, 62*(5), 446–464.

Anderson, L., & Stillman, J. (2013). Student teaching's contribution to preservice teacher development: A review of research focused on the preparation of teachers for urban and high-needs contexts. *Review of Educational Research, 83*(1), 3–69.

Anyon, J. (1997). *Ghetto schooling: A political economy of urban educational reform*. Teachers College Press.

Arends, R. I. (2001). *Learning to teach* (5th ed.). McGraw Hill.

Ashton-Warner, S. (1963). *Teacher*. Simon & Schuster.

Ball, D. L., & Cohen, D. K. (1999). Developing practice, developing practitioners: Towards a practice-based theory of professional education. In L. Darling-Hammond & G. Sykes (Eds.), *Teaching as the learning profession: Handbook of policy and practice* (pp. 3–32). Jossey-Bass.

Ballenger, C. (1992). "Because you like us": The language of control. *Harvard Educational Review, 62*(2), 199–208.

Ballenger, C. (1999). *Teaching other people's children: Literacy and learning in a bilingual classroom*. Teachers College Press.

Ballenger, C. (2009). *Puzzling moments, teachable moments: Practicing teacher research in urban classrooms*. Teachers College Press.

Ballenger, C., & Rosebery, A. (2003). What counts as teacher research? Investigating the scientific and mathematical ideas of children from culturally diverse backgrounds. *Teachers College Record, 105*(2), 297–314.

Berkshire, J., & Schneider, J. (2020). *A wolf at the schoolhouse door: The dismantling of public education and the future of school*. The New Press.

Berkshire, J., & Schneider, J. (2024). *The education wars: A citizen's guide and defense manual*. The New Press.

Berry, B., Daughtrey, A., & Wieder, A. (2010). *Teacher leadership: Leading the way*. Center for Teaching Quality. https://eric.ed.gov/?id=ED509719

Boostrom, R. (1998). "Safe spaces": Reflections on an educational metaphor. *Journal of Curriculum Studies, 30*(4), 397–408.

Bowers, C. A., & Flinders, D. J. (1990). *Responsive teaching: An ecological approach to classroom patterns of language, culture, and thought*. Teachers College Press.

Bryk, A. S., & Schneider, B. (2002). *Trust in schools: A core resource for improvement*. Russell Sage Foundation.

Bullough, R. V., Jr. (1994). Digging at the roots: Discipline, management, and metaphor. *Action in Teacher Education, 16*(1), 1–10.

Burleigh, R., & Wimmer, M. (2009). *One giant leap*. Philomel Books.

Butchart, R. E., & McEwan, B. (1998). *Classroom discipline in American schools: Problems and possibilities for democratic education*. State University of New York Press.

Cambone, J. (1994). *Teaching troubled children: A casy study in effective classroom practice.* Teachers College Press.

Canter, L., & Canter, M. (1992). *Assertive discipline: Positive behavior management for today's classroom*. Canter & Associates.

Carini, P., & Himley, M. (Eds.) (2000). *From another angle: Children's strengths and school standards.* Teachers College Press.

Carpenter, T., Franke, M., & Levi, L. (2003). *Thinking mathematically: Integrating artihmetic and algebra in elementary school.* Heinemann.

Carter, K. (1993). The place of story in research on teaching and teacher education. *Educational Researcher, 22*(1), 5–12, 18.

Castanheira, M. L., Crawford, T., Dixon, C., & Green, J. (2001). Interactional ethnography: An approach to studying the social construction of literate practices. *Linguistics and Education, 11*(4), 353–400.

Charles, C. M., & Senter, G. W. (2008). *Building classroom discipline* (9th ed.). Pearson/Allyn and Bacon.

Clandinin, F., & Connelly, D. J. (1988). *Teachers are curriculum planners: Narratives of experience*. Teachers College Press.

Clark, C. (1990). What you can learn from applesauce: A case of qualitative inquiry in use. In E. W. Eisner & A. Peshkin (Eds.), *Qualitative inquiry in education: The continuing debate* (pp. 327–338). Teachers College Press.

Cochran-Smith, M. (1991). Reinventing student teaching. *Journal of Teacher Education, 42*(2), 104–118.

Cochran-Smith, M., & Lytle, S. L. (2009). *Inquiry as stance: Practitioner research for the next generation.* Teachers College Press.

Cochran-Smith, M., Villegas, A. M., Abrams, L., Chavez Moreno, L., Mills, T., & Stern, R. (2015). Critiquing teacher preparation research: An overview of the field, part 2. *Journal of Teacher Education, 65*(5), 109–121.

Cohen, B. (1994). *Thank You, Jackie Robinson.* HarperCollins.

Cohen, D. (1988). *Teaching practice: Plus ça change . . .* Michigan State University, National Center for Research on Teacher Education.

Cohen, D. (2011). *Teaching and its predicaments.* Cambridge, MA: Harvard University Press.

Dewey, J. (1909/1978). *John Dewey: The middle works. 1899–1924* (Vol. 6). Southern Illinois University Press.

Dewey, J. (1938, 1998). *Experience and education.* 60th anniversary edition. Kappa Delta Pi.

Diamond, J. (2008). *Welcome to the aquarium: A year in the lives of children.* The New Press.

Doyle, W. (1986). Classroom organization and management. In M. C. Wittrock (Ed.), *Handbook of research on teaching* (3rd ed., pp. 392–431). Macmillan.

Duckworth, E. (1987). *"The having of wonderful ideas" and other essays on teaching and learning.* Teachers College Press.

Duke, D. L. (1979). *Classroom management.* National Society for the Study of Education, distributed by University of Chicago Press.

Edwards, C., Gandini, L., & Forman, G. (1998). *The hundred languages of children: The Reggio Emilia approach—Advanced reflections* (2nd ed.). Ablex Publishing.

Epstein, J., & Sheldon, S. (2023). *School, family, and community partnerships: Preparing educators and improving schools* (3rd ed.). Routledge.

Erickson, F. (1986). Qualitative methods in research and teaching. In M. C. Wittrock (Ed.), *Handbook of research on teaching* (3rd ed., pp. 119–161). Macmillan.

Featherstone, J. (1995). Letter to a young teacher. In W. Ayers (Ed.), *To become a teacher.* Teachers College Press.

Feiman-Nemser, S. (1983). Learning to teach. In L. Shulman & G. Sykes (Eds.), *Handbook of teaching and policy* (pp. 150–170). Longman.

Feiman-Nemser, S. (2001). From preparation to practice: Designing a continuum to strengthen and sustain teaching. *Teachers College Record, 103,* 1013–1055.

Fenstermacher, G. (1990). Some moral considerations on teaching as a profession. In J. I. Goodlad, R. Soder, & K. A. Sirotnik (Eds.), *The moral dimensions of teaching* (pp. 130–151). Jossey-Bass.

Fenstermacher, G. (2001). On the concept of manner and its visibility in teaching practice. *Journal of Curriculum Studies, 33*(6), 639–653.

Fenstermacher, G., & Soltis, J. (1986) *Approaches to teaching*. Teachers College Press.

Fries, K., & Cochran-Smith, M. (2005). Teacher research and classroom management: What questions do teachers ask? In C. Evertson & C. Weinstein (Eds.), *The handbook of research on classroom management* (pp. 945–981). Erlbaum Publishing Company.

Gallas, K. (1994). *The languages of learning: How children talk, write, dance, draw, and sing their understanding of the world*. Teachers College Press.

Gallas, K. (1998). *"Sometimes I can be anything": Power, gender, and identity in a primary classroom*. Teachers College Press.

Giebelhaus, C. R. (1994). The mechanical third ear device: A student teaching supervision alternative. *Journal of Teacher Education, 4*(5), 365–373.

Ginott, H. (1972). *Teacher and child: A book for parents and teachers*. Macmillan.

Gonzalez, L., & Carter, K. (1996). Correspondence in cooperating teachers' and student teachers' interpretations of classroom events. *Teaching and Teacher Education 12*(1), 39–47.

Good, T. L., & Brophy, J. E. (2003). *Looking in classrooms* (9th ed.). Allyn and Bacon.

Goodlad, J. (1979). Perspectives on theory, research and practice. In D. L. Duke (Ed.), *Classroom management*. National Society for the Study of Education, distributed by University of Chicago Press.

Grant, C., & Tate, W. (1995). *Multicultural education through the lens of the multicultural education research literature.* https://eric.ed.gov/?id=ED382704

Greene, M. (1978). *Landscapes of learning*. Teachers College Press.

Greene, M. (1993). Diversity and inclusion: Toward a currciulum for human beings. *Teachers College Record, 95*(2), 211–221.

Greene, M. (2001). Reflections on teaching. In V. Richardson (Ed.), *The handbook of research on teaching* (4th ed., pp. 82–89). AERA.

Halaby, M. (2000). *Belonging: Creating community in the classroom*. Brookline Books.

Harvard-Smithsonian Center for Astrophysics, Producer (1987). *A private universe*. https://www.learner.org/series/a-private-universe

Hole, S. (1998). Voices inside schools—Teacher as rain dancer. *Harvard Educational Review, 68*(3), 413–422.

Jennings, L. B., O'Keefe, T., & Shamlin, M. (1999). Creating spaces for classroom dialogue: Co-constructing democratic classroom practices in first and second grade. *Journal of Classroom Interaction, 34*(2), 1–16.

Johnson, S. M., & The Project on the Next Generation of Teachers. (2004). *Finders and keepers: Helping new teachers survive and thrive in our schools*. Jossey-Bass.

Kingon, J. G. (2001, April 8). A year in the trenches. *New York Times*, 30–38.

Kohn, A. (1996). *Beyond discipline: From compliance to community*. ASCD.

Kohn, A. (2021, September 22). The 25 year case against the classroom management field. *Education Week*.

Kounin, J. S. (1970). *Discipline and group management in classrooms*. Holt, Rinehart and Winston.

Kovalik, S. (1997). *Integrated thematic instruction: The model* (3rd ed.). Susan Kovalik & Associates.

Kraus, R. (1971). *Leo the late bloomer*. Scholastic.

Krechevsky, M., & Stork, J. (2000). Challenging educational assumptions: Lessons from an Italian-American collaboration. *Cambridge Journal of Education, 30*(1), 57–71.

Lakoff, G., & Johnson, M. (1980). *Metaphors we live by*. University of Chicago Press.

Lampert, M. (1985). How do teachers manage to teach? Perspectives on problems in practice. *Harvard Educational Review, 55*(2), 178–194.

Landau McEwan, B., & Stollenwerk, D. A. (2000). *The art of classroom management: Effective practices for building equitable learning communities*. Merrill.

Lave, J., & Wenger, E. (1991). *Situated learning: Legitimate peripheral participation*. Oxford University Press.

Lawrence, J. (1995). *The great migration: An American story*. Harper Collins.

Le Fevre, D., Timperley, H., Twyford, K. & Ell, F. (2020). *Leading powerful professional learning: Responding to complexity with adaptive expertise*. Corwin.

Lewis, C., Perry, R., & Hurd, R. (2004). A deeper look at lesson study. *Educational Leadership, 61*(5), 18–22.

Lieberman, A., & Miller, L. (2005). Teachers as leaders. *Educational Forum, 69*, 151–162.

Lortie, D. C. (1975). *Schoolteacher: A sociological study*. University of Chicago Press.

Malaguzzi, L., & Gandini, L. (1998). History, ideas and basic philosophy: An interview with Lella Gandini. In C. P. Edwards, L. Gandini, & G. E. Forman (Eds.), *The hundred languages of children: The Reggio Emilia approach—advanced reflections* (2nd ed., pp. 49–97). Ablex.

Marshall, H. (1990). Metaphor as an instructional tool in encouraging student teacher reflection. *Theory Into Practice, 29*(2), 128–132.

Martin, J. R. (1992). *The schoolhome: Rethinking schools for changing families*. Harvard University Press.

McNally, J., & Menter, I. (2009). Teacher learning and development in the UK. *Teaching and Teacher Education, 25*(7), 941–943.

McNamee, T. (2007). *Alice Waters & Chez Panisse: The romantic, impractical, often eccentric, ultimately brilliant making of a food revolution*. Penguin Press.

Meier, D. (1995). *The power of their ideas: Lessons for America from a small school in Harlem*. Beacon Press.

Meier, D. (2002). *In schools we trust*. Beacon Press.

Meier, D. R. (1997). *Learning in small moments: Life in an urban classroom*. Teachers College Press.

Miletta, A. (2010). Learning by doing: A year of teacher research. In A. Campbell & S. Groundwater-Smith (Eds.), *Connecting inquiry and professional learning in education: International perspectives and practical solutions*. Routledge.

Miletta, M. (1996). *A multiage classroom: Choice and possibility*. Heinemann.

Montessori, M. (1964). *The Montessori method*. Random House.

Noddings, N. (2001). The caring teacher. In V. Richardson (Ed.), *The handbook of research on teaching* (4th ed.). AERA.

Paley, V. G. (1979). *White teacher*. Harvard University Press.

Paley, V. G. (1984). *Boys and girls: Superheroes in the doll corner*. University of Chicago Press.

Paley, V. G. (1992). *You can't say you can't play*. Harvard University Press.

Peacock, J. L. (1986). *The anthropological lens: Harsh light, soft focus*. Cambridge University Press.

Perrone, V. (2000). *Lessons for new teachers*. McGraw Hill.

Peterson, R. (1992). *Life in a crowded place: Making a learning community*. Heinemann.

Pratt, C. (1948). *I learn from children: An adventure in progressive education*. Simon and Schuster.

Ravitch, D. (2010). *The death and life of the great American school system: How testing and choice are undermining education.* Basic Books.

Richardson, V. (1988). *How teachers change.* http://ncsall.net/index.html@id=395.html

Richardson, V. (2003). The dilemmas of professional development. *Phi Delta Kappan, 84*(5), 401–406.

Richardson, V., & Fallona, C. (2001). Classroom management as method and manner. *Journal of Curriculum Studies, 33*(6), 705–728.

Richert, A. (2012). *What should I do? Confronting dilemmas of teaching in urban schools.* Teachers College Press.

Rodgers, A. (2012). Supervision 1.3: Leveraging trends in teacher preparation and supervision to address 21st century issues in the United States context. In A. Cuenca (Ed.), *Supervising student teachers: Issues, perspectives, and future directions* (pp. 169–190). Sense Publishers.

Rodgers, C. R. (2002). Seeing student learning: Teacher change and the role of reflection. *Harvard Educational Review, 72*(2), 230–253.

Romano, R. M. (2000). *Forging an educative community: The wisdom of love, the power of understanding, and the terror of it all* (Vol. 126). Peter Lang.

Rosebery, A., & Warren, B. (1998). *Boats, balloons, and classroom video: Science teaching as inquiry*. Heinemann.

Sarason, S. (1999). *Teaching as a performing art.* Teachers College Press.

Schwab, J. (1978). *Science, curriculum, and liberal education: Selected essays.* University of Chicago Press.

Sinclaire, C. (1994). *Looking for home: A phenomenological study of home in the classroom*. State University of New York Press.

Slavin, R. E., & Madden, N. A. (1999). *Disseminating success for all: Lessons for policy and practice.* Johns Hopkins University, Center for Research on the Education of Students Placed at Risk.

Slavin, R. E., Madden, N. A., Dolan, L. J., & Wasik, B. A. (1996). *Every child, every school: Success for all.* Corwin.

Sockett, H. (1993). *The moral base for teacher professionalism*. Teachers College Press.

Starratt, R. J. (1990). *The drama of schooling / The schooling of drama.* Falmer Press.

Taba, H. (1962). *Curriculum development: Theory and practice.* Harcourt, Brace & World.

Tuohy, D. (1999). *The inner world of teaching: Exploring assumptions which promote change and development*. Falmer Press.
van Manen, M. (1986). *The tone of teaching*. Heinemann.
Westheimer, J. (2009). Learning among colleagues: Teacher community and the shared enterprise of teacher education. In M. Cochran-Smith, S. Feiman-Nemser, & D. J. McIntyre (Eds.), *The handbook of research on teacher education: Enduring questions in changing contexts* (3rd ed., pp. 756–784). Routledge.
Zeichner, K., & Liston, D. (1996). *Reflective teaching: An introduction*. Lawrence Erlbaum.

Resources

Social Studies

National Council for the Social Studies: https://www.socialstudies.org

Southern Poverty Law Center: https://www.splcenter.org

Learning for Justice (formerly Teaching Tolerance): https://www.learningforjustice.org

Maya Lin: https://www.mayalinstudio.com/memory-works/civil-rights-memorial

Storypath: https://www.socialstudiesk8storypath.com

Social Studies School Service: https://www.socialstudies.com

Mathematics

National Council of Teachers of Mathematics: https://www.nctm.org

Development and Research in Early Math Education: https://prek-math-te.stanford.edu

Lesson Study at Mills College: https://lessonresearch.net

Science

National Science Teaching Association: https://www.nsta.org

Annenberg Learner—A Private Universe: https://www.learner.org/series/a-private-universe

Children and Nature Network: https://www.childrenandnature.org

The Edible Schoolyard Project: https://edibleschoolyard.org

Language Arts

National Council of Teachers of English: https://ncte.org

National Association for Bilingual Education: https://nabe.org

National Writing Project: https://www.nwp.org

Parents and Teachers

Network for Public Education: https://networkforpubliceducation.org

National Parent Teacher Association: https://www.pta.org

National Network of Partnership Schools: https://nnps.jhucsos.com

NEA Foundation: http://www.neafoundation.org

Carnegie Foundation for the Advancement of Teaching: https://www.carnegiefoundation.org

Going Public With our Teaching: http://www.goingpublicwithteaching.org

Jennifer Berkshire and Jack Schneider: https://www.haveyouheardpodcast.com

Alfie Kohn: https://www.alfiekohn.org

Children

Reggio Children: https://www.reggiochildren.it/en (city's website in Italian with many links and resources, publications: http://www.scuolenidi.re.it/index.jsp)

North American Reggio Emilia Alliance: https://www.reggioalliance.org

Hampshire College Institutes on Descriptive Inquiry and Descriptive Process: https://sites.google.com/idiprocess.org/idi/about-us

Prospect School and Center for Research and Education Archives, University of Vermont: https://scfindingaids.uvm.edu/repositories/2/resources/882

National Association for the Education of Young Children: https://nyaeyc.org

Index

About the Author

Alexandra Miletta, PhD, is a former elementary teacher and teacher educator who teaches prospective and practicing teachers at the graduate level and works in predominantly urban contexts. In 2008 she published with her mother, Maureen Miletta, *Classroom Conversations: A Collection of Classics for Teachers and Parents*, and has published and presented research on classroom climate, teacher education, and practitioner research. She currently lives in Rome, Italy.